Praise for *Advice From Your Trans Aunty*

"This book is a gem. It's a sound book of advice delivered with a big, open heart. Vogel is contributing to the queer community's rich history of elders passing down our earned knowledge of survival and joy, and she does it with warmth, wisdom, and a deep sense of care. She's writing to and for every trans person bravely facing the world as their truest self."

Cody Daigle-Orians, They/Them, creator of Ace Dad Advice and author of *I AM ACE*

"Erica Vogel has produced a moving, poignant, and informative collection of stories and anecdotes together with powerful advice that shares not only pieces of herself with her audience, but dispenses nuggets of wisdom and empathy that any reader would benefit from, no matter their life circumstances or identity. I learned much, but was also deeply moved. I felt like an old friend was speaking to me over coffee, sharing their life and knowledge with me. It was a privilege to read."

Sophia MacLennan, She/Her, Trans Social Media Influencer

Advice From Your Trans Aunty is a warm, insightful, and incredibly valuable resource for anyone navigating the complex journey of gender transition or questioning. As a transgender man myself, I found Vogel's guidance to be practical and deeply affirming. Vogel writes with the casual, comforting tone of a wise and caring relative, making even the most daunting aspects of transition feel manageable. Her anecdotes add authenticity and humor while never overshadowing the advice she offers. The book covers an impressive range of topics, from the early stages of gender questioning to the nuances of workplace transitions and long-term advocacy. Vogel's emphasis on self-love and finding joy in one's authentic identity is compelling. Her repeated assertion that there's no single "right way" to be trans is refreshing and validating. One of the book's greatest strengths is its balance of emotional support and practical guidance. *Advice From Your Trans Aunty* is an essential read for anyone questioning their gender, beginning transition, or seeking to understand transgender experiences better. It's the supportive, informative guide I wish I'd had when starting my transition journey."

Liam Paschall, He/Him, Transgender Speaker, DEI Trailblazer, LinkedIn LGBTQIA Top Voice

"*Advice From Your Trans Aunty* provides accessible and actionable recommendations for anyone looking to explore their gender. Erica speaks to the reader like a friend and offers her own perspective as a trans woman with a complex and beautiful background in living."

Leo Caldwell, He/Him, Transgender Educator

"Erica Vogel's insightful book is one that I wish I had been able to read when I was a young trans person seeking answers to the millions of questions I had about gender identity, coming out, transitions, the workplace, advocacy, and other trans-related stuff. Her advice is sound. Her experiences are valid. And her desire to help others is evident on every page. I cannot recommend this book highly enough. Read it, friend, for you will surely learn one or maybe many things you never knew before."

Vanessa Sheridan, She/Her, National Transgender Consultant, Keynote Speaker, and Author

"In her own words, Erica aims to "give people information that enables their growth, education, and agency." *Advice From Your Trans Aunty* does exactly that and brilliantly so. If you have any questions at all, whether about your own journey or that of someone you love, this book is for you. Erica addresses everything from questioning to advocacy, offering guidance from her own experience as well as from stories she collected along her journey. Everyone should have a trans aunty who imparts this kind of wisdom and now, thanks to Erica, we all can!"

Amelia Michael, They/Them, Workplace LGBTQIA and Gender Inclusion Author, Trainer, Speaker, & Consultant

"*Advice From Your Trans Aunty* is a must-read for anyone seeking a deeper understanding of the transgender experience. This book goes beyond surface-level explanations, offering a raw, honest, and deeply empathetic look at the emotional and practical aspects of transition. As a business professor, I often emphasize the importance of empathy in leadership. This book is a powerful example of how empathy can be fostered through storytelling. Vogel's personal experiences and insights create a space for readers to connect with the challenges and triumphs of being transgender in a profound way."

Anastasia Thyroff, PhD, She/Her, Associate Professor of Marketing, Clemson University

Advice

Trans
Aunty

Advice

FROM YOUR

Trans

Aunty

Erica Vogel

Publish
Your Purpose

For permission requests, write to the publisher, addressed "Attention: Permissions Coordinator," at the address below.

Publish Your Purpose
141 Weston Street, #155
Hartford, CT, 06141

PYP **Publish**
Your Purpose

The opinions expressed by the Author are not necessarily those held by Publish Your Purpose.

Ordering Information: Quantity sales and special discounts are available on quantity purchases by corporations, associations, and others. For details, contact the author at info@ericavogel.com.

Edited by: Nancy Graham-Tillman
Cover design by: Erica Vogel and Rebecca Pollock
Cover Photograph by: Lauren Barkume
Typeset by: Jet Launch

ISBN: 979-8-88797-125-4 (hardcover)
ISBN: 979-8-88797-124-7 (paperback)
ISBN: 979-8-88797-126-1 (ebook)

Library of Congress Control Number: 2024912066

First edition, January 2025.

Publish Your Purpose is a hybrid publisher of non-fiction books. Our mission is to elevate the voices often excluded from traditional publishing. We intentionally seek out authors and storytellers with diverse backgrounds, life experiences, and unique perspectives to publish books that will make an impact in the world. Do you have a book idea you would like us to consider publishing? Please visit PublishYourPurpose. com for more information.

DEDICATION

To my wife, my person, my love, my best friend.
Melissa, without your love and support, none of this
would have been possible.

Thank you to my kids and family for participating
in this wild journey.
Your love, support, and acceptance have made
all the difference.

DISCLAIMER

Some names of individuals have been changed or omitted to protect their privacy.

CARE WARNING

While this book is informative and light in many places, some topics mention self-harm, suicidal ideation, and sexual abuse. While these topics are covered at a high level, even mentioning them may cause some to experience difficulty.

CONTENTS

CHAPTER 1

FAMILIARIZING

Welcome to *Advice From Your Trans Aunty,* an advice column in a book. As such, each chapter focuses on broad topics aligned by category, and each contains many of the questions I've been asked to give advice on throughout my life. This first chapter includes questions I've fielded about myself and my background to help you understand who I am and where I'm coming from.

Let's dive right in.

WHAT DO I KNOW, ANYWAY?

Who I am now did not suddenly show up when I turned 50 and transitioned. I'm a grizzled tech veteran of twenty years; I barely survived the dot-com bubble, multiple start-ups, and several Fortune 500 corporations. I've seen up close the rise and fall of companies, and I've seen some real corporate shit go down. I've hired hundreds of people, had to lay off and fire people, and been laid off thrice myself. With equal ease,

I've navigated countless conversations with both front-line employees and CEOs and even designed digital experiences that are now being used by 75 million people over four billion times a year.

I've also dealt with financial struggles lasting almost a decade and a half when I struggled to pay the rent and put food on the table. I'm still paying off student loans from one of my degrees. My parents never prepared me for a life of financial responsibility, and I had to figure it out the hard way through making many mistakes. My mom was a surgical nurse, then a medical recruiter, and is a recovering alcoholic. My stepfather was domineering, imposing, and a coke addict. My father was only somewhat in the picture, and when I did see him, I watched him struggle with life as a gay man in the AIDS crisis of the 1980s and '90s.

I spent my early childhood in the Southern Baptist church, where I learned that I was not indeed a girl and that it was deeply sinful for a boy to think otherwise. During this time, I was molested repeatedly by an elder of that church, who was my great-uncle. Eventually, I escaped multiple years of abuse when my family moved from Florida back to my birthplace of Atlanta, Georgia.

After struggling with school as a young graphic designer, parent, and husband trying to make my way in the world, I dropped out of college. I was already deep into therapy at this point and knew that not only was my life not working, but my gender was confusing me at times, which made me uncomfortable; I tucked it away as deeply as I could.

As I continued to maneuver through life, I conquered problem after problem after problem while also working on my childhood and sexual abuse traumas. I eventually learned not to get fired from jobs, and I found stable work that got me beyond paycheck-to-paycheck living, creating a career by bootstrapping my way up over 15 years. I raised kids, one of whom almost died from bacterial meningitis, and another had four surgeries by the time she was 15. Another child made me a grandparent by the time they were 18 and then came out as trans five years later. My oldest child is estranged due to our difficult relationship.

At age 49, I experienced the worst physical pain in my life with a severe back injury that left me bedridden for four months and caused me to rapidly lose 20 pounds due to my being unable to eat through the pain. Through the remainder of that year, my health slowly improved, but my ability to push my gender dysphoria to the back of my mind disappeared. My fear of honestly dealing with my dysphoria, moving forward with my transition, and talking to my family about it brought me to the brink of self-harm and death.

I have seen a lot and lived life with many highs and lows. Today, I'm thankful to be married to a wonderful queer cisgender woman, and together we are raising her son. My kids are exploring their world as adults, my career has taken off, and I have the wherewithal to write this book. I speak from hard-earned experience, grit, resilience, and love of myself and those around me. These qualities and the love and support I've received along the way helped me navigate my world and get to where I am today.

WHAT IS THIS BOOK ABOUT?

The transgender community was built on oral tradition, where passing on information to others is incredibly common. Fortunately, this has made the nuts and bolts of transitioning relatively easy to find, particularly online. And most of us who've been around for a while have found a trans big sister, brother, or sibling who points us in the right direction, such as where we can find information on the ideal blood volume of estrogen for feminization, legally changing our name, or gender marker change laws and guidelines in a given area. We can easily find answers to many of our questions because sharing information is what the larger community excels at. I've rarely looked hard to find information pertinent to my transition needs.

But what if you want to know how to interview for a job as a transgender or nonbinary person or how to come out at work? What if you have questions about medical advocacy or want to know how to pay it forward to new trans people? Life gets tricky when questions like these come up.

I'm frequently asked for advice on life in the transition process. This book explores ways of thinking about how the problems related to the process impact you. I've based the questions on the issues I've been repeatedly asked about, and this has given me the opportunity to form collective and thoughtful answers and responses. Some of the knowledge in this book comes from more than just my thinking; it's information that has been passed anecdotally from person to person in the community, with my daily experiences layered on top. I ask that you approach these questions and answers with an open mind and be willing to look at not only how others impact your life but also how you impact your life and others. This will require you to do some self-investigating at times. And while there is advice on how to work with other people here, the goal is to help you find yourself and be that person out in the world.

The information in this book is directional, and in no way is it written from the perspective of things you *must* do. I am not you. I have not lived your life, nor do I live in your town or have your family. I cannot speak about your specific situation, but I can provide a point of view to consider. However, it's up to you to decide whether that view will benefit your life. Pick up what makes sense and leave the rest behind.

You should know that I consider all angles before making a decision, which can take time; however, once I make a decision, I take immediate action. If I wait, I'll consider something for days, weeks, months, or years, only to come back to the same answer. I throw myself into things with both feet because I'd rather take a chance at improving things than worry about being wrong. I know I can get through anything; I've already proven that to myself many times. But I've softened my can-do attitude throughout this book, as you may not operate that way.

Though my day job is in technology, my gay job is advocating for the LGBTQIA community, with a strong focus on the transgender and nonbinary experience in and out of the workplace. In that role, I speak at conferences, sit on a nonprofit trans board, write articles, mentor others, plan employee resource group (ERG) events, am a member of many Discord servers, and maintain an online presence. Often when speaking to groups of people, I field questions like the ones in this book.

Before we go further, I must discuss my rationale for writing this book. I actively work to remove racism from my thoughts and actions, a pursuit that will take the rest of my life. I'm a feminist, and I was raised by a mother who's also a feminist as well as a civil rights and women's rights activist. I firmly believe I cannot work to advocate for the transgender community without also advocating for *all* marginalized communities. As such, I have to acknowledge the privilege I have. I've been fortunate to live in the metro area of one of the queerest cities in the United States: Washington, DC. Living near a liberal megacity has afforded me the ability to go to an excellent transgender clinic for all my care. Being employed in the tech field, I earn an income that makes the transition process accessible, if not easy. I'm also White and have a graduate degree. Though I'm in a stable position today that many in the transgender and nonbinary communities are not, you'll soon learn that has not always been true for me.

My transness and my sexuality are what primarily marginalize me. My status and my presentation are undeniably transgender. I pass as transgender and not as a woman or a man. I'm also 5′ 11″, built like a retired athlete, and have big, blond curls. I get clocked everywhere I go. Still, I have more privilege than most. Yet I aim to lend as much of that to others as I can for the rest of my life. I'm a work in progress, and I hope this book meets the bar I set for myself. However, I suspect in some areas I've fallen short. I welcome being called out in those situations.

I've spent much time working out my demons, battles, and mistakes, which have cost me greatly. It takes work to look inward and critically review the life you've created, but you can do it. Here are some keys to making that a bit easier:

1. Give yourself and others grace because we all fuck up.
2. Pay attention to how people show and tell you who they are the first time; that's when they're most honest with you.
3. Let go of regret because if you dwell on the past, it continues to be your present and future. Go back and deal with how you feel so that you can LET IT GO.
4. You do not owe *anyone* the benefit of sitting around and taking their bullshit. No healthy form of love requires you to take abuse from people.
5. Give yourself and those you love time to process and work through stuff.

WHY ME?

When I came out to life as a medically transitioning transgender woman at age 50, I was working as a senior product manager at a large US bank. I hoped to lead a happy, trouble-free, and quiet life as a trans woman finally free of crippling dysphoria. I wanted peace and a calm mind—a simple, anonymous life.

I recall telling my first trans big sister that I could never be a firebrand like her. At the time, she was the coleader of the trans arm of the LGBTQIA ERG where I worked. She was the first trans person I'd ever spoken with at length. She was outspoken, "loud" as she put it, and a strong advocate for trans and nonbinary people in and out of work. I admired her. She listened to my statement and said it was perfectly fine to lead a quiet life as trans and that many people choose that path. With a twinkle in her eye, she relayed that if I ever wanted to use my voice, I should let her know. I know now she saw who I was far better than I did.

As weeks passed, she helped me plan my coming out at work, introduced me to other trans and nonbinary people, and encouraged me to engage with my peers. My coming out went incredibly well, and I was blown away by the outpouring of love and acceptance I received from over 200 people the day I published my letter announcing myself at work.

A few months later, that voice my big sister mentioned started showing up. I was quite astonished to find myself mentoring people, speaking up, and helping develop programming for the community at work. I was then asked to speak on a panel at the Out & Equal Workplace Summit in Las Vegas. As part of my day job, I regularly represent my work in front of crowds, and by this point I'd spoken at conferences, presented speeches, and given thousands of presentations. I'm a storyteller in my job, so speaking at a summit wasn't intimidating to me.

I was amped to speak on this panel on the first day of a three-day conference, and my energy was through the roof. I usually experience a bit of nerves that resolve when I get in front of a crowd, but this time I was full of excess energy; I was giddy. I told my story and was candid, funny, and warm, as though all the people were my friends instead of strangers. This panel went astronomically well, was one of the conference's highlights, and was mentioned in several subsequent panels.

I spent the remaining time at the summit being stopped by person after person in the conference center, in restaurants, on the street, in the airport bathroom on the way home, and then online in the following days. I was shocked; this was not at all what I expected. I assumed I'd do my thing, enjoy three days of the conference, chat with a few people, and go about my life.

One thing was clear: I loved showing up for my trans and queer fam, and if my voice could help, I was damn sure I was going to use it. As I walked the corporate halls of advocacy, I had many opportunities to listen to others, offer my point of view, check on people, and do what I could to make life a bit easier for LGBTQIA people in and out of work. I wrote articles and blog posts, appeared on podcasts, hosted events, mentored other associates, worked on the national leadership team of the LGBTQIA ERG at work, and helped lead the DC area chapter. I also spoke outside of work, donated my time and money, and mentored many people. I discovered my voice was most potent in speaking to the transition process.

WHY A BOOK?

I always had a way with words, speeches, presentations, conversation, and the like. Through my voice, I connected with people. I had so much to say. Yet something was still not right. Not authentic. Then, I finally decided to transition to my true self: Erica. Like many others, as a transgender person I always felt less than myself, incomplete, or unreal. This is not to say I didn't have times when I was entirely me or real; I did. But this little voice always told me, "You're fake."

As I grew confident in myself, living fully out as trans, I found that voice getting quieter and quieter. It's still there in dark corners, in places of anxiety or regret. Mostly, though, it stays quiet now. While struggling with wanting to write a book but not having a goddamn clue what to write about, my friend Shikka told me to stick to my strengths and write about the advice I'm asked to give so often. Hence, *Advice From Your Trans Aunty* was born.

WHY DO YOU DO THIS WORK?

I do this work because I want trans and nonbinary people to thrive and have meaningful yet regular lives. When I look out at the landscape and hear from person after person, "What do I do now?" I can't help but remember how hard it was to find voices I trusted in my transition. This book is the result of being asked repeatedly for advice on trans issues that are far more about life than they are about the specifics of name and pronoun changes or medical plans.

When I hear day after day, "How do I talk to my family?" or "How do I meet other trans and nonbinary people?" I remember that I felt the same way. In the beginning, I too had so many questions, and the ones I could find answers to had little to do with thriving as trans. This book offers support, advice, and direction for your life, now and in the future. Being that I'm a trans woman, my perspective is naturally rooted in that experience. However, I have come to know and count on many friends in the nonbinary and transmasculine community and take measures to speak broadly about all experiences whenever possible.

Ultimately, I want you to hear, know, and feel that who you are is worthy of love and respect. You are a vital and valid member of the trans, nonbinary, and queer community. The pursuit of authenticity you're on is the most beautiful example of casting off what isn't true so that you can become the best version of yourself. Transition is the ultimate leap of faith and the ultimate act of self-love. Remember, you must continue to love yourself on this journey because it's the best guidepost for navigating life.

CHAPTER 2

EVALUATING

If you're unsure whether you're transgender or nonbinary or are currently evaluating your gender, this chapter is for you. Before we dive in, please know there is no *one* way to be trans and no prerequisites from life to move forward. Remember, no one can make this decision for you. It is up to you, dear reader, to take your first step.

CARE WARNING:
Some topics below mention self-harm and suicide.

ARE GENDER AND SEXUALITY LINKED?

Despite what you may believe, gender and sexuality are not linked. This misplaced association comes up regularly, so I'm starting with this question. Let's define three terms right up front, with credit to the Human Rights Campaign for using their versions.

1. Gender expression: external appearance of one's gender identity, usually expressed through behavior, clothing, body characteristics, or voice, and which may or may not conform to socially defined behaviors and characteristics typically associated with being either masculine or feminine.

2. Gender identity: one's innermost concept of self as male, female, a blend of both, or neither—how individuals perceive themselves and what they call themselves. One's gender identity can be the same or different from their sex assigned at birth.

3. Sexual orientation: an inherent or immutable enduring emotional, romantic, or sexual attraction to other people. Note: an individual's sexual orientation is independent of their gender identity.[1]

Many people outside the trans community confuse sexual orientation and gender, assuming the two are linked. This misunderstanding leads to many trans people being asked about their sexuality when they come out. The truth is, though many see their orientation persist, some in the period of profound exploration and uncovering of truths about themselves due to transition might see their orientation expand, and some may see their orientation move entirely in the other direction. There are a lot of theories on this, but the one that resonates with

---

1. Human Rights Campaign, "Glossary of Terms," last modified May 31, 2023, https://www.hrc.org/resources/glossary-of-terms; Human Rights Campaign, "Sexual Orientation and Gender Identity Definitions," accessed June 20, 2024, https://www.hrc.org/resources/sexual-orientation-and-gender-identity-terminology-and-definitions.

me is that a significant change in orientation has to do with comfort with the self and comfort with sexual discovery, both of which become unblocked in the process of transition. That said, there's a beautiful representation of nonbinary people, trans women, and trans men who are straight, bi, pan, queer, asexual, lesbian, or gay as viewed from the perspective of their gender. This reinforces the fact that gender and sexuality are not linked. As we go forward, we'll continue to challenge these assumptions and deconstruct the narratives that tell us that being transgender is not okay.

HOW DO I KNOW WHETHER I'M TRANSGENDER?

How to know whether they're transgender is a common question almost every transgender and nonbinary person has likely fretted over. They Google, read up on the topic, ask trans friends, or contact prominent community members online for their opinions. Not all, but most dwell on this for a while, seesawing back and forth in the "am I or am I not" category.

While I can't answer this question for you, I can point you to a good indicator: the "Am I Trans?" Rubric. To be clear here, I am not offering a professional opinion, nor am I a therapist or a doctor. What I'm offering is a simple guide built upon what I've seen many others use in the past as well as my own experiences talking with people. Most importantly, please view your responses as further rationale to speak with a gender specialist who can answer your questions more fully with their professional guidance. With those potential hazards identified, let's move on.

The "Am I Trans?" Rubric

1. **Part One: Give Yourself One Point for Seriously Wondering Whether You're Trans**

    Why: Cisgender people rarely think about their gender other than abstractly, which amounts to how they feel about themselves in their world. "I am a woman, wife, and mother who is a tech product manager and loves *Star Wars* and coffee in equal measure" is a statement that typically fits smoothly into their worldview, and they're facts that require little additional thought because they naturally align with their gender. Cis people don't dwell on their gender, and even if they're attracted to the opposite sex, they generally experience a mild aversion to the idea of *being* that gender.

    DISCLAIMER: Thinking "men have it better" (because they do in patriarchy) does not make you trans. There's a difference between the injustice of societally enforced status and being transgender. There's also a difference between not liking aspects of your body as a woman or a man and not feeling at home in your gender. Similarly, feminine men and masculine women are not in denial if they feel at home in their bodies and gender expressions.

2. **Part Two: Give Yourself One Point If the above Is a Persistent Feeling after You've Realized It's There**

   Why: Gender incongruence persists. Being transgender is not a short-term affliction you can catch. Yes, we're hella cool. No, we can't make anyone *be* transgender. This feeling of dis-ease (dysphoria) lasts as long as you feel your gender expression does not match your core self. Awareness of this feeling since childhood is not a requirement; simply that it persists over months or longer without abating is enough. Be aware that this feeling can also come and go depending on your ability to stuff it back in its box.

3. **Part Three: Give Yourself One Point If It Feels Right When You Try It On**

   Why: Try on a name, pronoun, or gendered clothing to see how doing so feels. No shaming yourself is allowed on this one. Be in the moment and see how you *feel* about the idea. It doesn't hurt to take it for a test drive. Imagine if someone called you Jane instead of John or Sir instead of Ms. or if you could wear that dress you saw without worrying about others' reactions. The goal is to treat this as if it were simply a fact that everyone knew and accepted as who you are without judgment or concern.

> If you score a 2 or 3, I suggest you talk to
> a professional to explore further.

I have to acknowledge that while this may seem straight-forward and simplistic to those who are not transgender, for people wrestling with the potential of being trans, it can feel drastically different. The reality is that you're likely dealing with anxiety, depression, dysphoria, and a general sense of dread for what this means in your life. The next step is to find a person you trust to talk to about what comes after.

There's a real likelihood that fear will talk you out of what you know to be true. Ask yourself this: if there were no repercussions, no negative actions that would follow, no loss of family, friends, status, income, or whatever the fear is telling you will happen, would you go forward as trans or not? The answer to that question will tell you a lot. You also can't erase what happened at conception, and if your rationale for not going forward is that you'll never be a "real woman" or a "real man," there may be fear and internalized transphobia you need to examine. I'm not saying you have to go forward, but it's worth looking into.

In this process, please take measures to be safe. Talk to people you trust, talk to a therapist, or call a harm prevention hotline if you need it.

IS IT TOO LATE TO TRANSITION?

No matter your age, it is never too late to transition. I often come across this question from people who are 20–80 years old. Typically, it's a question we ask ourselves to gate-keep our transness. I find two thought processes in play when I come across this topic. The first I find with people 40 and older, and it's genuinely a question of whether it's worth it at this point in their lives. Resoundingly and unequivocally, yes, it is. There is never an age too old to transition; there is never a time too late to live your truth. For Gen X and older members of the community, we grew up with the worst messaging about trans people, and it can be hard to overcome the awful tropes we see portrayed in the media again and again. It's very likely you've internalized transphobia you need to sort through. Take the time to challenge your notions and understand why you believe it may be too late.

Though I knew for much of my life, I was too afraid to move forward. I thought I had "cured myself" of being trans, but it kept coming back. Eventually, the transition process became a necessary step for me to take. And I wasn't a teen or in my early 20s; I was 50. I'm here to tell you that every day since then has been a blessing. I should've done it sooner, but I wasn't ready. I couldn't stop gaslighting myself that I didn't need to transition, that it wasn't real for me, or that I was "cured." Did I lose time? Of course. Does it matter in the end? No, because I'm here now, and it took my whole life up to this point to be ready for it.

If you're worried about the results of medical transition, no matter what age you are, know there are no guarantees. Yes, some things might be easier when living less time in a body running on the wrong hormones. Don't let fear and influencers in the media tell you it's too late for you. There is never a time in your life that is too late to be your best self. And if your rationale for not moving forward is your looks, that's internalized transphobia talking to you.

The second thought process has more to do with the boom in trans social media influencers who generally fit very nicely into what society thinks of as "acceptable" transgender people: White, young, and pretty trans women. Let's be honest here,

White trans women, of which I am one, get the lion's share of attention and the majority of the limited acceptance the community receives. But so many sectors of transness deserve our focus. The representation we seek out must include Black, Indigenous, and other people of color (BIPOC) because their experiences and voices are not only vibrant and beautiful but also central to the trans advocacy movement. Until this group of trans people can step forward in society, none of us will.

Trans men come in various ages and presentations and are some of the most incredible people I know. They play a vital role in the community, particularly in the healthy masculinity they embody. Nonbinary people cover a wide range within the community and are at the forefront in terms of breaking down harmful barriers and expectations of gender roles. I count many nonbinary people as friends, and I certainly would not be the person I am today without them in my life. You cannot have a true sense of the trans experience without including all these groups, and you'd be doing yourself a great disservice by ignoring them. Seek out voices from all areas of transness, not just the ones that represent you.

People considering transition consume any info they can find, and often, what they come across first are the people with the most followers. Don't get me wrong, many of these people are great community ambassadors who have my full respect. However, not all are good people, and some cause a lot of problems. A complicating factor is that many people who are just starting to explore their gender may not know people in their real lives who are trans, so they haven't had the opportunity to learn from their elders about the problematic stance some community members take.

One of the most damaging narratives this group promotes is ageism-focused messaging. I cannot tell you how many times gender-exploring people have asked me with their hearts in their throats if they are too old to transition at 20 years old. What a wild thing that is to hear. This is directly a result of the dangerous narrative perpetrated by some people who had the privilege to transition younger and then started up the mean girl game trying to make the club exclusive. Every time I see the effect this has on people, I become furious. Please be aware that these ideas cannot be further from the truth and are always rooted in personal gain over community responsibility. These messages come from trans people who use very narrow definitions to disenfranchise as much of the community as possible. They believe that only those who've had all the surgeries count as trans people. And if you're non-binary, you're nonexistent as far as they're concerned. We'll hit on this topic in more detail later.

Either way, no matter your age, circumstances, means, or method you want to follow in transition, no one can tell you it's too late. As soon as you hear anything like that, please know you are listening to extremist groups in the trans community.

AM I TRANS ENOUGH?

The "Am I trans enough?" question is usually asked in private, with a heart in the throat and the loaded fear of being excluded. I usually get this one from two perspectives. The first is "Should I transition?" which is about gatekeeping the self before moving forward. The second is "Do I fit in?" with the transgender or nonbinary community, which is about seeking acceptance.

I cannot state loudly enough that there is no threshold of being transgender or nonbinary that you need to cross to be "enough." Who you are right now is trans enough. Medical intervention, legal name change, and being out is not required. What *is* required is that you know yourself.

If you see things from the first perspective, you're worried whether you're trans enough to move forward. You've concluded that you're "trans-ish" and taken the point of view that there's a line in the sand you need to cross first. Many people have relayed to me their versions of the line in the sand, which have included "I still misgender myself," "I don't have a new name in mind," "I don't want to have surgery," and "I don't feel dysphoria strongly." Some even use "I don't have suicidal ideation" as a rationale for wondering whether they're trans enough.

When debating my transness, some part of me knew, but another part of me tried desperately to distract myself from this fact. I had to let that voice get loud and dangerous before I listened to it. However, this did not stop me from debating with myself and trying to find a reason not to go forward. Meanwhile, I was dealing with deep anxiety, fear, depression, and thoughts of self-harm. I questioned myself because I didn't want a vaginoplasty and sometimes felt more nonbinary than trans. I thought my life was perfect. I kept using thoughts like *Why would I mess this up?* and *Maybe I'm just a feminine man* as reasons I shouldn't go forward. All of these, along with self-hate in terms of being cruel with myself when my transness came to the forefront, were my fears speaking louder than my own knowing. Meanwhile, my mental health was plummeting; my fear was causing me so much harm.

Dear trans sibling, you are trans enough. Take a step forward because as soon as you do, you will know for sure one way or the other. Nothing permanent is going to happen in the beginning. Even hormones will take time to make permanent changes, but you'll likely feel improved mental health quickly if transition is for you. By the end of my second week on hormones, I knew I'd made the right choice. Take a chance on yourself because you're worth it.

Moving on to perspective two, "Am I trans enough?" (to fit into the community). Oof! I get this one a lot. It usually comes with some version of "I'm not like the others; is that okay?" I've been asked this because people felt they were not enough of an advocate, not out publicly, not loud enough, not far enough along in living their truth or transition, not pretty or handsome enough, and a hundred other worries. It seems to come up in comparison to someone who lives openly, people who pass as trans, and those in a position of authority in the community.

I also went through a period like this, and it still occasionally shows up. One factor at play here is confidence in who you are. Your authenticity—your very sense of being—is a crucial aspect to focus on and sort out. You can only be yourself; that is the only you worth being. You did not go through all of this to try to be like someone else. You've spent years trying to be what society told you to be. Don't fall into that trap again.

The other factor here may be the people you're spending time with. If you aren't exactly like them, it will be okay. If your group is trying to enforce the idea that you need to meet specific criteria to be one of them, then you need to consider whether that's the right group of people to be with. The trans community is generally quite accepting, but that doesn't mean every part of the community is.

You are trans enough for any sector of the community where you feel alignment. If others disagree, they're missing out on the best parts of you.

WHERE CAN I FIND RELIABLE INFO ABOUT BEING TRANSGENDER?

It might seem surprising, but I've encountered many transgender or nonbinary people who have yet to find reliable information. This situation is particularly true regarding medical care; many in the community rely solely on what they hear from peers and friends. Peer information can be excellent, but you must remember that not everyone has the same results and experiences and some advice is not universally applicable.

A good Google search should connect you to meaningful data; however, here are some trustworthy sources I like to recommend:

- **The Gender Dysphoria Bible**: https://genderdysphoria.fyi/en

  This is a wonderful resource covering the mental, physical, and emotional aspects of being transgender for men, women, and nonbinary individuals broadly. It's an excellent resource for those who are questioning, friends and family, and allies, and it's a good primer on dysphoria, transition, and what to expect. While written by a trans woman, it has excellent information for all under the trans umbrella.

- **World Professional Association for Transgender Health (WPATH) Standards of Care**: https://www.wpath.org/soc8

  This is the governing medical care document for transgender people in the United States and is followed by many other countries as well. Fair warning: this document heavily uses medical terminology, and reading through it can be quite a tough slog at over 200 pages. However, it's an essential read for anyone considering medical treatment as a part of their transition.

- **The National Center for Transgender Equality**: https://transequality.org/

  This is an excellent site for and about trans people. The site covers fundamental questions, laws, travel advisories, and advocacy information that impact the trans community.

- **The Trevor Project**: https://www.thetrevorproject.org/

  This is an excellent advocacy resource for transgender people and allies.

- **PFLAG** (formerly Parents, Families, and Friends of Lesbians and Gays): https://pflag.org/

  This is a resource for families of LGBTQIA individuals and has local chapter information. It's an excellent resource for education and support groups.

There are loads of books in publication to consume as well, and they run the gamut from education to advocacy to memoir. While I've read many of them, I recommend you seek the ones that match your tastes and interests.

WILL HORMONE REPLACEMENT THERAPY WORK FOR ME?

After "Am I trans enough?" hormone replacement therapy (HRT) may be the most common subject I receive questions about. We all go into this step with a lot of trepidation because we have little idea what our results will be. Does HRT work? Absolutely!

HRT is a complicated topic, and although I'm well-informed about it, I'm not in a position to be the source of truth. Please refer to the excellent info on the Gender Dysphoria website at genderdysphoria.fyi for a great summation of this topic. Outside of understanding how HRT works, two items come to mind when I get this question: the worry the person asking the question has going into HRT, and the impatience for the results; it takes years to bring about the full effects of HRT.

Let's talk about HRT jitters first. HRT provides a wide range of effects that are impacted by your genes' ability to make them manifest. From conception, our DNA has the codes for both male and female development built in. HRT is effective because those genes can work with whichever signal they receive. With a change in hormones, our genes receive the message to express themselves in the "appropriate" direction:

feminization for nonbinary femmes and trans women taking estrogen, and masculinization for nonbinary mascs and trans men taking testosterone. Trans women will take on the secondary sex characteristics of cis women, and trans men will take on the secondary characteristics of cis men. There will also be an impact on reproductive organs. Trans women will grow functional breasts, have reduced body hair, go through redistribution of facial and body fat to feminine patterns, develop a reduced ability to achieve erections and produce sperm, and more. Trans men will grow facial hair, add muscle mass, increase body hair, develop a deeper voice, increase body heat, change body odor, and may see their menstrual cycle reduce or stop. Both will experience an improvement in mental health as their brains start running on the correct hormone. The correct hormone sent to the brain can have a transformative change in depression, anxiety, and dysphoria.

Everyone starting HRT feels nervous. We hope for the best, but honestly, it's a leap of faith that we hope will pay off. With regret rates at only 1–2 percent for gender-affirming HRT, I think it's fair to say the vast majority of people see improvement in their dysphoria and mental health. You need to have a little faith and patience. I recall hoping HRT would help me but setting low expectations to protect myself. Initially, upon taking my first doses of estrogen, I noticed no changes and started to worry it wasn't working for me. However, the first sign became apparent after two weeks and was not what I expected: The noise in my brain stopped cold. I'd always had this static in the background, and it suddenly dissipated after two weeks on estrogen. That's when I knew HRT was working for me. This new, clear-headed feeling told me all

I needed to know. I had always suspected that my primary problem with dysphoria centered on the testosterone my brain was receiving. I went from being an old car with a tank full of cheap gas to a high-octane sports car with premium gas meant just for my brain.

Relatively quickly, other common feminizing HRT signs started showing up, such as nipple soreness that told me breast growth had started, reduction in nocturnal erections, and more. I couldn't know then how well my body would respond over a few years, which leads me to the issue of impatience for the results. HRT is a marathon, not a sprint. While you will see noticeable changes in your first year, you will also notice changes even after five years. You have to be patient. You cannot rush through this process no matter how strong a dose of HRT you take. HRT is the messenger, and sending an all-caps message will not make your genes work faster. I frequently remind people how long puberty took the first time around, a good two to five years, with many people seeing subtle changes well into early adulthood. For example, most men can only grow decent facial hair starting in their 20s.

While not all people respond predictably, all people experience the effects of HRT. Most will experience satisfaction to a great degree if they look back after a few years. For those who still want more or faster change than HRT provides, surgery then becomes the option of choice if available and affordable.

As long as you go into HRT knowing that it's a multiyear process for full effect and being realistic about what it can and cannot do, you will find that it did you good.

WHAT IS YOUR TRANS AND QUEER ORIGIN STORY?

My origin story is not a topic I get many questions about, but there is an exercise I find helpful to unpacking some of the baggage we all carry, especially the kind society has handed us about being transgender or queer. There is no better time to start than when you're considering or are early in transition.

If you've seen any superhero or action movie, you know they invariably start with the main character's origin story. Two people I admire, Theresita Richard and Deena Fidas, both of whom are DEIB executives, developed the exercise to help connect us with our origins of thought around our sexual orientation and gender identity. The goal of the exercise is to gain awareness of what we know to be true about ourselves and what we may have internalized from outside anti-LGBTQIA sentiments. We want to find what makes our humanity come to the foreground.

Origin Story Exercise

Before you start, grab a pen and paper to write with or a computer, tablet, or phone to type on.

1. When did you first learn about LGBTQIA people, and how were they referred to at that time? You might have heard derogatory language used as a joke or slur, or you may have heard about the community in favorable terms. Take some time to think back.

I grew up in the southeastern part of the United States, was a child of divorced parents by the time I was three, and had a father who was somewhat out as gay. I have no memories of my father in a straight relationship. I grew up mainly in Atlanta, a very queer-friendly city. I also spent six years living in Florida, where on Wednesdays and Sundays we went to a Southern Baptist church, typically an unwelcoming place for the community. I heard gay slurs throughout school, mainly because my dad was gay. Kids assumed my father had AIDS even though he didn't. However, I never hid who my father was. I wasn't ashamed, and I knew that if I came to the conclusion that I was gay, I'd be just as whole as anyone else. While I experienced hate, I also experienced how loving and kind the queer community is because of my father's partners and friends. Two of my friends in high school were out and were ostracized for it. I learned that my transness was sinful, wrong, less than, and something to either cure myself of or smother away into dark places deep down. These experiences are all part of my origin story.

2. What words describe your feelings when considering your origin story? They can be positive or negative.

My words are *resilience*, *love*, and *cruelty*.

3. To unleash your superpowers, what do you need to release? What keeps you from being your most authentic superhero self, even if your origin story is positive?

I needed to release the idea that I had to be impressive, a good trans spokesperson, pretty, passing, and quiet, as well as the concepts of being broken, a problem, and too much for people.

4. Release these expectations and limitations to claim your freedom from "should" and "not enough" thought processes. You are strong, beautiful, handsome, queer, and/or trans beacons of humanity. Remember, just because somebody told you these things about yourself, you do not have to keep carrying them. Put them down so you can lift yourself up. Write them down on a piece of paper, then wad that paper up and throw it in the trash. You may have to do this often until your expectations and limitations stay in the trash for good.

As you go forward, please continue to unpack the garbage you were handed in life and told was more valuable than the best parts of you. At your core, who you are cannot be something anyone else owns or approves of. It is yours alone.

IS THE NAME I CHOSE FOR MYSELF GOOD?

Whenever I get asked whether a community member's chosen name is good, it throws me off my stride. I always think, *Why would you come to me to ask whether the name you chose is good? Who am I to judge?* Over the past few years, I've reflected on this and concluded that we feel cautious because we're used to naming others, not ourselves. From that lens, it may be natural to crowdsource a new name. I'm not an expert on names, nor do I have any authority to tell you whether the name you're considering is right. However, I'll relay my advice.

Choosing a name can be quite a debilitating exercise. I made this easier for myself by setting some boundaries for guidance. As someone who has difficulty deciding, I made three rules that helped me narrow the list: (1) it couldn't be a name shared with someone I knew well and still interacted with because I worried that might look like I was taking their name, (2) my name should be age appropriate; as a child of the 1970s, I wanted a common name at the time of my birth and to try to land on something my mom might have chosen, and (3) I would find a way to honor a family member with my name because I knew that was a choice my mom would make. The end goal I focused on was landing on the name I might have received had all involved known I was a girl.

Following this simple rubric, I narrowed my list down to three names I liked, of which Erica was one. The actual decision came down to what felt right at the moment my therapist asked what she should call me. Interestingly, Erica was my third choice, but it's the name I blurted out. Today, I don't recall the other names I was considering. Erica stuck, and it feels very much like home to me at this point.

Even so, I was unsure of the name and decided to ask my mom what she had planned as a girl's name. She had told me the name years prior, but I could not recall it for the life of me. So when I asked this question after coming out, she got excited in assuming I would take up the original name she had planned. Dear reader, the name was Marinella (mare-eh-nel-ah). I burst out laughing because I was sure my mom was joking; she has a great sense of humor, so I thought this was a bit. She was not kidding, and things got really awkward. She intended this name to combine her adored mother's and favorite aunt's names. I couldn't do it; I could not take this name. "Marinella" wasn't me, and I knew I would've gladly shortened it to Mary or Ella in school had I been given that name as a child.

Still wanting to honor family members somehow, I pivoted to my grandmother, whom I never met. My grandmother Mary was an army nurse in WWII, serving in a MASH unit, and was supposedly the first woman in the US Army to be injured in the line of duty. I can't find any info to confirm that, but I have an excellent photo of her on a hospital flight with many soldiers that was used in *Life* magazine during the war. She met my grandfather, a naval lieutenant serving alongside John F. Kennedy, while she was caring for him in the hospital after his injury. Sadly, she died of breast cancer when my mom was thirteen. Grandma Mary is my mom's hero. Mom also went into nursing to follow in her mother's footsteps, despite my grandfather insisting she become a literature professor like he was. My mom was a damn good nurse and worked alongside some of the best surgeons for years. I know she made Grandma Mary proud. Ultimately, after being raised on my grandmother's legend, I chose a play on her name as my middle name, which made my mom very happy.

Finally, I used my partner's last name in the process because I never felt connected to my father's name. My wife is my person, and I knew her last name would do very well for me. She didn't take mine because she's a feminist badass with a PhD and a published author who proudly chose to keep her last name. My name fits me so well; I adore it.

Please feel free to use a version of this method or develop your own. No matter your rationale, the name that feels right or sounds like home when people say it is the right name for you.

HOW DO I HANDLE REGRET AND RESENTMENT ABOUT THE PAST?

I hear a lot from people who are struggling with regret over not starting transition sooner. You might be saying, "Erica, it seems a bit early to talk about the past." But I want to talk about it now because regret can color so much of the trans existence. I want people to start working on it early because these issues can only dissipate if we face them.

First, I want to call out the difference between regret and resentment. Both have roots in dwelling on the past and may involve the same feelings of anger or sadness. Once you get started with the transition process, you may find you begin to feel regret over waiting so long to start. Or you may feel resentment over the uncontrollable circumstances of your conception and the resulting cascade of development and hormones that led to the sex you were assigned at birth, which doesn't match your gender. These feelings are common and can cause a sense of lost time, opportunity, and agency. My loving reminder to you is to be gentle with yourself.

The past is immutable, but how we feel about it is not. Transition is initially all-consuming and is physically, emotionally, and mentally challenging. Do not let the past keep you from the present. Your choice to wait was rooted in your limited ability to see transition as a viable option, which we all come to in our own time and way. While we can't change the circumstances of conception, we can work to love who we are now. I spent a lot of time wishing I'd been born in the right body and that the world would see me as the girl I was. I prayed every night for God to set things right the next day and change my body.

My definition of regret is dwelling on past events for which I had agency but should've made better choices. In other words, I made lousy decisions and now have to live with them. My definition of resentment is dwelling on past events for which I had no agency or power to affect the outcome. In other words, something happened *to* me and now I have to live with it. I try my best to live life with no regret and no resentment. That means when I feel either of them, I take action to resolve them because, rather than them serving me going forward, they rob me of feeling like my life is my own.

Regarding regret, I often sort through why I should've made better choices, which can be painful. Auditing our past decisions is a minefield, but it's worth learning to walk through. Our past decisions, whether good or bad, led to us being the people we are today. Review the past with a heavy dose of grace, and apply what you learned to the current version of yourself, with a big focus on self-forgiveness. Unresolved regret equates to hundreds of pounds of extra weight you carry with no benefit to who you are now.

Resentment is a different flavor because it's all about what was done to you by another. Though I'm big on forgiveness, dealing with resentment isn't easy for me. When I spend time being angry about something from my past that can't be changed, I'm torturing myself. The "gift" of happenings and traumas from other people stays with you. Reclaiming the part of yourself that you feel someone else still possesses is a critical component in moving on from resentment. For me, I either address that person, walk away from them, or both. No matter my course of action, I reclaim myself from them so that I no longer have to give emotional and mental space to their actions. My life belongs only to me, and when I feel resentment and let it persist, someone else still owns a part of me. I will not let that stand.

When I was 28, I walked out of my dad's life. He was not active in our relationship, and he repeatedly chose not to know much about my life. I was solely responsible for our parent–child relationship for ten years. One day, I walked away, stopped calling, and didn't go to his business or house. He never attempted to track me down. I moved out of state and eventually sent him a letter telling him what had happened and why. He apologized but admitted he was unlikely to drive the relationship due to how his personality worked. We went 15 more years without speaking a word to each other.

As we both got older, I knew that at any time he might pass, and suddenly I couldn't help but feel regret. I dwelled on it for a year, talking myself out of reaching out to him. I finally realized how much energy I was putting into regret and chose to email him. Is the relationship better? Mildly. Do I have regrets at this point? Not at all. I was feeling regret because I felt I owed myself one last go at the relationship so that when he passed I wouldn't forever feel like I could've made a different choice.

Identify your regrets, face them, and resolve what is causing you angst, because your peace of mind is worth it.

CHAPTER 3

BECOMING

Now that we've covered the "Holy shit, I think I'm trans" part of the conversation, let's move into the "Now what?" section, or as I call it, becoming your whole self. This chapter dives into some, but not all the considerations and situations you should prepare for in transition. We'll focus on the things I and many others wish we'd known before we started. I hope you come through this chapter feeling more informed and ready to begin this part of your journey. There are too many options for me to discuss them all, so please take this chapter as more of a guide than a step-by-step walkthrough.

IS TRANSITION WORTH IT?

A million times over, yes transition is worth it! I know being a trans and gender nonconforming person is hard and that the perception of us is at an all-time low. However, I would not trade who I am now for anything, and that sentiment is shared by so many of us. Would we like the world to be kinder, more accepting, and less punitive? Would we like the world to treat us like humans who are just getting through the day like everyone else? Yes, of course. Though we're in difficult times, my life is still better than it was by a mile. It's harder in some ways, but it's better in many others.

My position lies firmly in the camp that being transgender is lovely and magical, even when it causes us more difficulty. I will not internalize the difficulty others force on us because of their intolerance, as if *I* am the problem. Trans people are some of the most courageous, resilient, and authentic people who've given up what society has forced them to be to become the best version of themselves. Society doesn't need to look to billionaires or Hollywood stars for inspiration; they should look to us. Who else takes the fantastic leap of faith we do to cast off what's crushing us to fling ourselves forward towards a better tomorrow?

Yes, transition was worth every damn second of my life that I now get to live. I would not trade this for *any* sum of money, even when it's hard as hell.

IS MEDICAL TRANSITION HARD TO NAVIGATE?

Talking about the medical side of transition is hard to build into a singular answer because there are too many paths to follow. I suggest you find people in the community who have experience in the care you're considering for yourself. However, I'm always willing to talk about life in the process. What surprised me the most was the administrative work I needed to undertake in transition. I spent far more time than anticipated organizing and seeking care approval than I did getting the actual care itself.

You'll first need to research both regional guidelines and national guidelines that apply to you as a trans person. This includes determining what care you can acquire, the process for approval to receive said care, creating a plan to pay for the care, and narrowing the options applicable to you. I live in the United States, where access to gender-affirming care is currently determined at the state level. I live in a state where informed consent is the rule for HRT. As a result, all gender-affirming care is "available" given I meet specific requirements. For surgeries below the belt, I would have to be on HRT for one year and provide two letters of recommendation from health professionals for a referral to the applicable doctor. For surgeries above the belt, only one letter, if any, is required. Availability does not mean affordability, however, so cost planning is also a must. And though I didn't need to have a mental health diagnosis, I did need to meet with doctors and go through the process of asking for HRT. For the one surgery I had, an orchiectomy, two letters of approval from mental health professionals were needed.

The second surprising thing was the average doctor's minimal amount of information on working with trans and nonbinary people. I've had to become far more informed than they are in order to guide my care. I do see a lovely transgender specialist whose knowledge is top-notch, but my general practitioner, dentist, and medical specialists for other medical issues know nothing about trans care. While all these doctors have been affirming so far, unfortunately, you never get to stop coming out as trans in the medical world. Be cautious of doctors who blame your HRT for other problems you may be experiencing. We call this "trans broken arm syndrome," and it has far more to do with bias than with being informed in any way about trans medical care. When you run across one of these people, change doctors ASAP.

While we're on the topic of medical advocacy, I have to state that because I'm a White woman, speaking up for myself is typically well tolerated by doctors, if not always welcomed. Though my initial trans specialist was dismissive and combative with me in my care, I was able to switch to a fantastic doctor. However, for my Black and Brown trans siblings, self-advocacy becomes a more difficult proposition due to the history of medical racism that still runs deep in the United States. I cannot imagine how much more difficult navigating medical care must be for our most marginalized community of Black and Brown trans femmes and women. The only suggestion I have at this time is to be as educated on the topic as you can be so that at least you'll know bullshit when you hear it.

I also recommend reading the WPATH's Standards of Care version 8 and any text you can find on HRT. I found the book *Testosterone, an Unauthorized Biography* by Rebecca M. Jordan-Young and Katrina Karkazis to be quite informative for learning how both testosterone and estrogen work in our system. Take time to understand the blood work process and the results you should seek in HRT. To the best of your ability, know the options and the process for surgeries you might choose, many of which are well-documented and easy to read up on. Trust your network of trans siblings to point you to good people to work with.

Keep in mind that the first few appointments may take some time to work through. You'll need to give a complete medical history to your endocrinologist, and you'll discuss the best HRT dose and delivery method, whether oral, gel, or injection. Blood work becomes a constant part of your life on HRT, with draws happening as much as every three months in the first two years. If you struggle with needles, you need to mentally prepare yourself for this new fact of life. Pace yourself because gender-affirming medical care can be draining emotionally, mentally, physically, and financially. I've needed to take breaks from periods of activity to recover from the effort involved.

Finally, don't be afraid of getting too much information from the community. The trans community, particularly those who've gone through medical care, are quite open about their experiences with medical transition. It may put you off initially, but you'll find the information you can glean from those who've gone before you incredibly valuable. Beginning the process of transition does not give you permission to be rude and bluntly ask someone invasive questions, but please ask if someone is willing to share their experiences with you.

I'll leave you this final thought: you must persevere through the process and build momentum because it takes a long time to get anything done.

DO I NEED TO KNOW MUCH ABOUT MY MEDS?

HRT will work even if you don't understand why, but knowing what your meds are doing helps you work with your doctor.

Learning how hormones work and what your doctor looks for in your blood tests will help you choose a better path forward. This is not a requirement but simply some good advice I received.

Early on, my doctor and I struggled to get my estrogen levels to the 250 pg/mL mark. Fortunately, my testosterone quickly plummeted to an almost undetectable amount. Still, though my doctor updated my oral dose every visit, my estrogen levels remained at 115 pg/mL, which is on the low side of the normal range of 50–350 pg/mL. Puzzlingly, I was experiencing good feminizing effects from HRT. We both became concerned when test results showed I was casting off too much of the estrogen in my system and passing it through my liver. I was also converting estrogen into estrone, typically seen in menopausal women, at double the average level. High estrone is an indication you're not using estrogen effectively. My oral dose was high and I was unable to use it fully, which caused my liver to overwork itself and my blood levels to drop to the low-average side. Yet I was developing nicely with good breast growth, redistribution of body fat, and more, and I felt great despite what the numbers were showing. Since my testosterone was nicely suppressed, we switched to weekly injections of estradiol valerate and suspended testosterone blockers. This was before my orchiectomy, or in plain language, the removal of my testicles. My estrogen level went up to 175 pg/mL but was still low by most people's standards, yet I had excellent feminizing results.

The reality is that I'm sensitive to estrogen and can't make use of higher doses. There's some fascinating information out there indicating that people with naturally low estrogen or testosterone are sensitive to the respective hormones and can't make use of higher quantities in their blood, so their bodies produce less of the hormone in question. Conversely, people with high levels of these hormones are insensitive to them and need more in their blood to do the job adequately. Understanding the information driving this helped me not worry that my estrogen needed to be at a high level, a common point of view in the community. Without this knowledge, I would've focused on a high dose that was bad for my health while having the same feminizing results I'm seeing on my current dose.

Frankly, it comes down to peace of mind. I like to know the science behind it so I know how to ensure my needs are met safely.

AM I TRANSITIONING THE RIGHT WAY?

How to transition is always a complex topic for me to speak about because I have to put away my notions of what transition looks like for me. My transition process is not a measuring stick for others to follow.

In my experience, this topic is rooted in questioning the authenticity of our gender expression and whether it matches the people we see around us. The ask behind the question is for reassurance from one of two angles: (1) what the person perceives to be how most people transition; it's a "Do I fit in with the others by transitioning this way?" question, and (2) the person is walking a path they feel differs from the "standard"; it's an "I feel I'm not exactly like others" question, and they may not be pursuing HRT, for example. There is no standard path in transition, which is the whole point I'm making. There is not a path you *have* to follow.

Take it from me, this is a relatively common concern. It primarily comes up because we all felt othered in the gender expression we felt compelled to take on by our social structure. So in choosing ourselves, we can forget that giving up being who we are not requires us to figure out who we are. As such, making inauthentic choices to fit in doesn't serve us. You are the only person who lives in your skin, and it's for only you to decide what your transition involves.

As you build friends in the community, you'll find a vibrant variety of trans expressions. It's essential to prioritize how you feel about your gender expression. Self-doubt is common among newer people on the journey, and many feel anxiety as they work to become comfortable with their new expression. This anxiety often leads to wanting affirmation from others and to fit in with your trans peers. Please find like-minded people to connect with and learn from. However, it's best to prioritize your truth over theirs. If there's one thing the trans community is, it's opinionated. Many opinions are coming your way, and not all of them will fit you.

I recall in my first year of being out and medically transitioning, many of my trans friends were telling me to get my consult for bottom surgery done so I could get a surgery date on the calendar as soon as possible. A few used very strong tones when telling me I'd regret waiting to schedule my appointment. But I had never once indicated I wanted bottom surgery. The idea came from a sense of community and looking out for me, but it overrode what I felt was right for my body. I expressed my concerns to my therapist about not being the "right" kind of trans girl if I was unsure about surgery. It took substantial self-reflection and guts to resist the urge to follow what my elders were telling me. To this day, I've felt no desire to have bottom surgery, and I'm so glad I listened to my truth. In time, I may choose that route, but not today and not soon.

There is no one way to be trans or nonbinary. No one look is required, no age too old. Just as there's an infinite number of ways cisgender expression can look, the same is true for trans people. Prioritize walking your own path because that's the only one that leads to happiness.

SHOULD I TRACK MY PROGRESS?

I recommend tracking your progress to anyone just starting medical transition. The slow pace of transition can make it hard to notice the more subtle signs, such as changes in your measurements, as well as the more obvious ones, such as breast development or voice pitch changes. And on days when dysphoria hits you hard, reviewing the changes you've tracked can remind you of the progress you've made. Additionally, the valuable anecdotal research our community can provide by tracking these details helps create a better future for those who come after.

When I started estrogen, I took every measurement I could think of, including the standard ones a tailor might take but also my upper arm, my calf circumference, and more. I updated them monthly and eventually slowed to quarterly after the first year. I noted any change in my HRT dose, recent lab work results, and the dates of each. I've shared my spreadsheet template with many people, and most have found it helpful.

I also tracked changes that weren't covered by measurements, such as crying more easily and my tattoos becoming less faded due to the more luminous skin I now have. If I noticed something that felt new and persisted for a few days, I added it to my sheet. I tracked changes in sleep patterns, mental well-being, emotional connection, face shape, breast soreness due to growth, scalp hair thickening, propensity to more frequent mood swings, skin smoothing, and places where my fat distribution changed. On top of keeping track of my measurements, I now have more than 50 separate signs that HRT has made changes to my body, mind, and emotions.

This "transition tracker" has become an excellent resource for reviewing what has changed from a quantitative and qualitative point of view. I can tell you almost to the day when I first felt nipple soreness or when there was less static in my head, and I can tell you when I lost 0.5 inches in height due to estrogen thinning out my muscles and tendons. I even used it to track social transitions and my coming out to family, friends, and coworkers. Furthermore, I tracked all aspects of legal transition, which helped ensure I updated every record I could. All of this made the organizational element of transition more straightforward to manage and plan.

Tracking the transition process is a valuable resource you can return to, like reading an old diary full of terrific data. It's a rewarding resource you can refer to for the rest of your life.

HOW DO I CHANGE MY WARDROBE TO MATCH MY GENDER?

Changing your wardrobe is an entirely personal choice. Whether going from male-coded clothes to female-coded clothes or vice versa or adding some of both to suit your nonbinary style, updating your wardrobe is a pretty standard activity in the trans community. However, please know that you don't need to change a thing if you don't want to. Be yourself first and foremost.

Changing the clothes we wear to affirm our gender is fantastic and drives euphoric feelings for so many of us. If you want to rock that suit or a little black dress, go for it. I love that what I wear feels like a reflection of who I am. I first wore a cocktail dress at the Human Rights Campaign National Dinner, where so many dressed in fabulous finery. Every time I see that elegant halter gown with its black flowers on white, I can't help but grin from ear to ear at the memory.

I love color blocking, so you'll rarely see me in a singular color from head to toe. I particularly love black, white, and neutrals as the bases of my wardrobe because they allow me to add a bold pop of color with a bright top or bottom. I'll usually top the look off with a leather or suede jacket or stylish blazer as well as some gold jewelry. I have a big personality, and my color-pop style with an edge matches me well. Since I'm a 5′ 11″ lady, I rarely want to look like a wall of pink and will work to break that up. I spent time looking for style ideas to build my look, which has paid off tremendously. However, it's a work in progress, and I've had to evolve my style as I found combinations that worked better than others. For instance, I've learned that palazzo pants look great on me and that maxi dresses fit me best, despite me initially not thinking they would. I also figured out that colors too close to my skin tone wash me out no matter how much I like them, and cool colors are a little easier for me to pull off than warm tones.

The point I'm making is that at first your choices will be hit or miss, and you'll likely be frustrated with what you find. Keep in mind that it takes most people a year of work to find their signature style.

For those getting ready to tackle wardrobe changes as well as those struggling with them, here is some guidance that has helped me:

- **Understand the measurement system of the clothing you're about to adopt.**

  Sizing for women's clothes is wildly different from men's. Men's tops are S–XL, with extended sizes readily available. Men's pants are sized first by waist circumference and then by inseam in inches, such as 36 x 32. These sizes are relatively reliable within brands; in fit, a size L T-shirt at Old Navy is nearly identical to a size L T-shirt at Macy's. By and large, men can shop without trying on clothes if they so choose. However, I recommend trying on clothes if you like a close fit and for style choices.

  Women's sizing is an entirely different world of sizes 0–18, with extended sizes sometimes available. This range is used for tops, pants, dresses, skirts, and jackets but these items can also be labeled as S, M,

L, XL, and beyond. These numbers mean different things within and certainly between brands, so the vanity sizing in women's clothes can be unreliable. In most cases, women's clothes require trying on. Unisex or gender-neutral clothes usually follow men's measurement systems.

To make this process easier to manage, take your body measurements, memorize them, and learn how they translate to the clothing size system you're about to enter. If you dig in a bit, many clothing sites will give measurements in inches and centimeters. Poor-fitting clothes look terrible on everybody, so take the time to find a good fit.

- **Understand your frame.**

  Trans bodies present unique, fascinating, and frustrating problems to solve. Trans women tend to have a longer torso than cis women, and trans men tend to have narrower shoulders than cis men, for instance. For women's clothes, body shape makes a difference in how clothes drape, mainly because the fabrics they're made with are woven from softer and lighter fibers. For men's clothes, draping is rarely a factor because they're more structured and generally made out of thicker materials; it's all about how the structure of the clothes accentuates the shoulders and creates a V shape. Understanding how your body shape and curves translate into new clothing systems will help you find a good fit and style that's easier to achieve.

- **Find a muse.**

  You've likely imagined your new look by this point. Find a style icon you identify with, and work to build a few similar outfits so you have some go-tos that feel like you. The goal to work towards is to find something that feels like an expression of you, such as an animal-print top or a cool blazer, and start to anchor your wardrobe around making these pieces sing. Be willing to change things up repeatedly until you find combinations that work.

- **Avoid spending big on statement pieces at first.**

  However tempting it might be to spend big on a dress or a suit, this rarely works out in the early transition stage. You're often left with an expensive, ill-fitting, or poorly styled item of clothing you seldom wear. Your tastes will evolve as you become more comfortable living as your true self. If you're on HRT, you'll find that your body will change over time, meaning some of these first items won't fit the same a year later. Get what you need, but save the big purchases until you know what works, what looks good, and what you can wear repeatedly. A statement piece is good only if it looks great, feels authentic, and gets worn regularly.

- **Audit your wardrobe.**

  You will likely roll your wardrobe over multiple times throughout the transition process, particularly if you're on HRT. Audit the pieces in your closet regularly and ensure they still work. This is another reason to hold off on making big purchases; your opinions will likely change as you become more comfortable wearing your new clothes. Be prepared for your tastes to change along with how your body changes. Changing out your wardrobe is costly, so pace yourself and work within your budget so it's manageable.

- **Dress for yourself**.

    Forget the rules or what others think, and wear clothes that make you feel good and reflect your authenticity. Your sense of style comes alive when you focus on wearing clothes and not letting them wear you. This means avoiding pieces that aren't you no matter how stylish they may be. Understanding why a cool jacket full of style would or would not work for your aesthetic is where you want to get to, which takes time and experimentation.

To close this section, I'll remind you to give it time. You've come to this point in your life dressing one way and are now learning a new path. You'll make mistakes that you'll look back on a few years from now and wonder what you were thinking. You might even be surprised that the aesthetic you land on differs from the one you thought you'd choose when you started down this road.

TRANSITION WILL SOLVE ALL OF MY PROBLEMS, RIGHT?

While I don't get the exact question of whether someone's problem will be fixed when they transition, I get many flavors of this general idea. Let's face it: being trans is a huge issue to solve whether you're working through how to move forward or grappling with the ramifications it will have on your life. The size of the mental, emotional, and physical impact being trans has on your life is casting a long shadow, but it's certainly not the only issue.

When asked this type of question, I typically give some background on myself to illustrate the point I need to make. So let's jump in.

While being trans was a long-running theme I tried to deal with and hold off until I couldn't, I had my fair share of other issues going as well. Despite being a decent student, I struggled with some subjects in school and with apathy. I had yet to figure out how I needed to learn, which resulted in some classes being easy and engaging and some being harder for me than they should've been. (I eventually realized I'm an experiential learner, meaning I need to see information in action.) At the time, I was just not cut out for school but was trying to suffer through. This situation left a mark on my psyche, particularly because I'm a grandchild and niece of university professors and a daughter of brilliant parents. The experience scarred me so deeply that it was two decades before I returned to college after my first attempt and finally earned my bachelor's and master's degrees. During my first attempt, I became a parent, and the pressure of raising kids, holding down a job, and going to school was just too much. I spent years unwinding my sense of failure from being a barrier to understanding it and applying the correct learning strategies.

Speaking of jobs, I was a terrible employee for the first few years of my design career. Though I dropped out of art school, I eventually made it into the ad design world on the strength of my portfolio. But I was arrogant and difficult to deal with. After losing that job, I had to reset and learn how to be a productive, team-playing employee. During this time, I was also working for next to no money, so the pressure to figure it out was high. I eventually learned how to design better, listen to my clients, and bring about the vision of others, not just my own. In time, I moved up to being a creative director and then VP of an agency, but I was also laid off twice in this period. After some hard self-evaluation prompted by a series of failures, I figured out that when I left my ego at the door, I was a damn good leader, and this transformed my career.

As all this was going on, I was also grappling with the fact that I'd never had any financial education. I was living below the poverty line, barely making it paycheck to paycheck. The littlest hiccup could cause me to miss rent or debate how much food I could get by on so my kids could get enough to eat. Life was hell. I filed for bankruptcy in my 20s.

Slowly, I learned from each disastrous lesson thrown in my path. I made a little more money and lasted longer without a layoff until finally, after a decade, I was not worried about missing rent. Eventually I built up emergency funds. I had to learn how to plan, pay bills on time, track expenses, and take care of clothes and cars so they'd last, I dragged myself out of poverty with better-paying jobs, and I learned how to clean up my credit and manage it responsibly. Today, I'm on my way to building wealth enough to retire before I die.

Still, I had to deal with residual trauma from sexual abuse at the hands of a church elder as well as mental and emotional abuse at the hands of other adults in my life. I spent years reclaiming the parts of myself stolen by people I was supposed to trust, and I worked my ass off to resolve all my problems and trauma, hoping it would "fix" my transness. While I set myself up for long-term success after some hard work, I couldn't escape being transgender. Though I transitioned later in life after battling more dysphoria-driven anxiety and depression, my previous growth meant that my entire focus could be on transition.

While your life may look different from mine and there's little likelihood that being transgender is the only thing you need to work through, being trans sure makes it a hell of a lot more complicated to sort through other issues. Don't stop working on yourself after transition. You've built good habits in self-investigation, so figure out what else you need to work on. I promise it will be easier than transition is.

WILL TRANSITION CHANGE MY PERSONALITY?

I always pause for a bit before answering questions about personality changes. This topic deserves a thoughtful response because blurting something out can do more harm than good. The short answer is yes and no. While I cannot speak on this professionally, as I'm not a behavioral expert, I can talk about what I've experienced within myself and seen in the people I know.

What I've witnessed and experienced can only be referred to as blossoming. When you start living your truth as trans or nonbinary, you're letting go of gendered aspects of your personality that never fit you well. In a genuine sense, you're lightening the load on your psyche. When less is weighing you down, more of you can come forward to take up space. It's like going outside to breathe fresh air in the spring.

I'm not so much different as I am more than I was before. I was always outgoing, fun, and personable. Those things didn't go away but became more authentic, as though I was turning up the stereo volume so I could hear the vocals and instruments better. I did give up acting and dressing like a guy, but otherwise I leaned into who I am at my core. I'm more in tune with my emotions and express them more freely, and I'm more affectionate and confident as well as happier and friendlier. I'm no longer trying to perform a gender that never fit. Indeed "new" behaviors have emerged, but to me they generally seem to have always been there; I'm just no longer suppressing them.

It's fair to say, however, that after transition, some people do take on new hobbies and change their speech patterns, gestures, or how they move. Their hobbies and interests may change, or they may finally feel free to pursue current interests. For some, new ways of behaving emerge as well. While I'm reluctant to say people become entirely different, I cannot deny that everyone changes some aspects of themselves during and after transition.

While on this topic, I want to point out some of what's at play in the worries that family, friends, or even you might have. Frequently, trans and nonbinary people are held to impossible standards when it comes to "gendered behavior." We simultaneously hear that the masculinity or femininity we're now expressing is "over the top and fake" and have any sign of the opposing trait used against us. We're both criticized for embodying the same gendered traits as our cis peers and punished for not doing it well enough. Gender performance, which everyone acts out, is learned from our culture, not built into our DNA. Criticizing me as a trans woman is criticizing cis women as well. The roles cis people play in terms of gender were handed to them and learned, and trans people are no different.

Think of it this way: if you were finally free of anxiety, depression, and the massive weight on your chest, what parts of yourself would emerge when given a chance to blossom? Losing this baggage isn't *changing* your personality but allowing it to thrive.

CHAPTER 4

RELATING

One thing you can count on in transition is that people will treat you differently. As such, all your relationships will change to some degree. It also has to be said that transition will impact how you relate to the people around you. Our coming out fundamentally changes the tone of every relationship, and while people may know us well, we become something they feel unfamiliar with, which is quite alarming for some. More often than not, grace and patience are needed on both sides for the relationship to survive.

Unfortunately, I have to talk about negative outcomes before discussing specifics of how to move forward. If you're dealing with rejection, hate, or cruelty, you should at least temporarily step away from that relationship. I know it's excruciating when it involves parents, partners, or close friends, but in the end, if they cannot support who you are, you need to work towards setting some boundaries while the process plays out. Always remember that setting boundaries and maintaining them is up to you; you can't force others to behave well.

Boundaries are there for you to care for your needs while the person in question works through their stuff.

That said, let's explore what to prepare for and what you might encounter as the people around you get to know the person you're blossoming into.

COMING OUT

When we tell people who we are, it's both terrifying and freeing, and we may experience a whole host of other feelings as well. The following prompts cover a few scenarios you may encounter when going through the process of coming out.

Partners

I want to start this topic by discussing my journey with my current wife. Though she and I are doing great today, my transition was a complex process for us to work through. We started dating at a time in my life when I truly felt I had finally solved my transgender "problem." While it would surface on the odd occasion, I could comfortably put it out of my mind and move on with almost no difficulty. I thought it had become little more than a curiosity I'd grown out of, so I said nothing to her. I'd been through a lot of therapy for a variety of issues and had solved many of the other problems that plagued my past as well. As such, I felt I could move forward in life as a cis man with little issue.

In the first few years of our relationship, we talked about almost everything in our pasts. Over this period, I disclosed my financial choices that had led to bankruptcy in my twenties; the sexual, mental, and physical abuse I'd dealt with as a child; my poor track record with higher education; and my early issues with keeping a job. I talked about what my then teenage kids were going through, my relationship with my ex-wife, and on and on. I wanted to make myself an open book and trust her to hold all of who I am, especially because she did the same for me. Despite what you might think, I was a pretty private person, so this was not an easy process for me to go through. I hid that I'd been dealing with being transgender, both because I thought I had cured it and because I was afraid this fantastic person would find this one thing was too much to work through with me. I was wrong to believe I had cured being transgender and to conceal that from her for years.

Unfortunately, these are the types of justifications we make and the deals we strike with ourselves to try to get through an incredibly difficult issue that seems unnavigable when, in fact, honest discourse is best. My desire to hide something that felt so shameful caused me to make decisions I regretted later in life.

Several years into our marriage, gender incongruence surged back to life. I struggled mightily to hold it at bay, but I couldn't. So I told her I thought I might be a nonbinary-leaning femme. It was such a struggle for us because it not only was a complete and utter surprise to her but was immediately apparent that I'd left this most critical piece out of every conversation we'd ever had. Understandably, she felt betrayed and lied to and had trouble trusting me, especially since it wasn't the only thing I withheld from her earlier in our relationship, unfortunately. While she certainly wanted me to be happy in my own skin, I self-ishly underestimated how deeply this impacted her, our relationship, and our families. I needed to make space for us to process this together, not on my own.

For two to three years, we wrestled with this topic on and off, trying to find a way through it. In addition, I started therapy again, also on and off. We fought, we cried, we tried to pretend it wasn't there, and we repeated that cycle every several months. Two huge problems were that I felt transition was impossible, and I had horrific guilt for putting her through all of this. But through it all, our love for each other anchored us.

Then, on December 12, 2020, I had a rapid onset of severe back pain that was genuinely the most intense and constant pain I have ever felt in my life, and I dealt with it daily for four months. It changed everything for me. I've broken five bones throughout my life, and my daily pain was more than any one of those. I dropped 20 pounds in a month because the pain was too much for me to eat well. After months of testing, we thought it might be cancer, and I legitimately feared for my life. The issue turned out not to be cancer-related and was ultimately fixed with a lot of physical therapy. It's been three years, and I'm still not back to full capacity.

That event effectively turned on the firehose about my being trans. Anecdotally, I heard from my therapist that periods of significant trauma tend to lead to trans people getting honest about their gender. I couldn't put it back in the box, and I became seriously concerned about self-harm while combating severe anxiety, depression, and dysphoria for the rest of 2021. I finally told my wife about my fear that I might hurt myself, and that was the final straw for both of us. We had a long conversation about what to do, and through a lot of tears, worry, fear for my mental health, and a thousand other difficult emotions, we decided together to proceed with transition. But this was just the first in a series of conversations we had about how to manage the transition for ourselves and our family.

It's been fucking hard and really humbling, but today we're doing well. We're tremendously committed to each other, willing to work hard to get through it, and engaged in multiple rounds of couples therapy. While our relationship may look great to outsiders and like the transition was no big deal, it was a huge deal. However, I can't write about our relationship without stating that I betrayed her trust. I understand I had my reasons and that no one outs themselves before they're ready. But the relationship we now have works because I'm willing to own that I didn't trust her with this part of myself, despite the fact that she came out to me as queer at the beginning of our relationship. I had to earn back her trust over time.

Coming out to your partner is scary. Most of us have no idea how it's going to go and as a result approach it with fear and trepidation. Yet at some point, we must come out to our partners. With that in mind, I have a few best practices to consider as you go forward:

- Be honest, and the sooner the better. You may know when you start the relationship, or you may come to know later. Either way, if you're aware that you might be transgender or nonbinary, talk about it with your partner as soon as possible.

- Prepare for the conversation by writing out what you need to say. Include as many details as possible, and explain why you feel this way. If you need to read the letter to your partner, do so, but please don't leave them a letter to read while you're away. Talk to them face to face or sit with them as they read. Every facet of transition requires courage and conviction, and this step is one of the first places you'll need to put these into practice.

- Be willing to have a discussion not so your partner can talk you out of it but so you can have a dialogue with them and make yourself clear. Remember, your being transparent does not guarantee they will understand. Also, be aware that this discussion doesn't happen in one sitting; you'll likely need to discuss it in depth multiple times.

- Have empathy, both because they deserve it and because you certainly desire it for yourself. I'm not saying to put up with abusive behavior; what I am saying is that no matter how shocked they may be, they deserve as much compassion as you do. They're hearing news that's likely rocking their world and bringing into question everything you've ever told them.

- Communicate your expectations for the relationship, particularly whether you intend to separate or wish to work through this with them. This will very much be on their mind. Intentionality goes a long way here. Be aware that you *both* must choose to stay together, which may take time for your partner to decide.
- Be patient and kind with each other. Most partners won't get on board in one conversation; they need time, just like you did while sorting this out for yourself.
- Though some do, other couples don't survive transition. You must prepare to choose between transition and your relationship if that unfortunate scenario occurs.

This conversation is heavy most of the time. Please take care of yourself and suggest your partner do the same. I highly recommend both of you seek counseling.

Family & Friends

As with coming out to your partner, you'll likely feel trepidation when coming out to your friends and family. I recommend starting with the friend or family member you feel safest with so you can hopefully gain an ally as you move forward with other people. When I came out, in the hope that their potential toxicity might not spread, I saved the most problematic people for last, and for me, that was family members. I also started with people I knew could keep their mouths shut. While I didn't talk directly to everyone in my more distant circle, I did speak one-on-one with my close friends and family.

Another option is to have someone you trust speak to others on your behalf. However, you will have to see or talk to many of those people at some point, and whether they address it or not, things might be weird the first time you see them. Like the situation with your partner, you need to prepare for dialogue during this step. Here are some best practices:

- Prepare for the conversation. Write out what you need to say, including pertinent details, and explain why you feel this way. I mostly spoke with people one-on-one over the phone, as almost none lived near me.
- Speaking of one-on-one, if you feel the conversation may go badly with telling multiple people at a time, you might consider approaching them one at a time. Numerous people asking potentially difficult questions simultaneously will make it very hard for you to say what you need to say.
- Again, be willing to have a discussion not so your friends and family can talk you out of it but so you can have a dialogue with them and make yourself clear. As with your partner, your being transparent doesn't guarantee your friends and family will understand, and they will need time to process. This is another discussion that doesn't happen in

one sitting, and you'll likely need to discuss it in depth multiple times.

- Be patient but also firm in your conviction. This conversation is not a debate on which people get to weigh in. It's an opportunity for them to be informed, show their support for you, and express their feelings. Be willing to have a dialogue and answer questions because it's likely they've never known a trans person. In the relationships you plan to maintain, this step goes a long way in working through difficulties.

- No matter how well the conversation seems to go, understand that their shock is likely in play and may be preventing them from fully expressing their thoughts. They may feel entirely unable to express full support or their full dissent. You'll likely need to have follow-up conversations when you repeat what you said the first time and answer questions they may have thought of since, and you'll likely need to do some educating on the trans experience. Again, unless they know other trans people, they're likely to have little grounding in the topic.

- Your family and friends may or may not affirm you. If that unfortunate scenario occurs, you must prepare to choose between your authentic self and your relationships.

The conversation will be heavy, and you must be prepared to care for yourself no matter how it turns out. Make sure you set up a check-in with someone you trust after the conversation. Be ready to leave the environment if it's in person and the conversation goes badly. But remember, if this is a relationship you want to keep, it's worth giving people time and space to process the news and learn how to support you.

Coworkers

Coming out at work is both similar to and entirely different from talking with family and friends. The information you share at work is usually less personal than what you say to the people close to you, and workplace environments have different spoken and unspoken rules than our inner circles.

When I came out, for example, I was working at a large financial services corporation with over 50,000 associates. A company of this size typically has a large LGBTQIA community, particularly in the banking world. My coming out started six weeks before I sent my letter to my coworkers. First, I contacted the lead of our transgender ERG to gain her support, then I spoke with my HR rep, and the ERG lead joined the call to help me convey my needs. The three of us began to plan what this process would look like. We talked with my boss and brought her into the planning, and together we compiled a list of more than 200 people to notify. We also spoke with the executive in charge of my division to seek her support. As we approached the day in question, I wrote a letter for my coworkers to read via email, which I reviewed with my ERG lead, my HR rep, my boss, and my executive. We planned for my letter to go out at 9 a.m. that Thursday, which coincidentally was International Transgender Day of Visibility.

As a fairly prominent person in my division, I interacted with hundreds of people and executives. I was about to become the second highest-ranking trans person in the company and the one in the most visible role, with my work known by C-suite individuals. There would be no way for me to go about my work life in relative anonymity. I was incredibly nervous about coming out to so many people at once, and my boss and executive were ready to reply instantly with a warm and welcoming message. My letter talked about my gender, my pronouns, my new name, and, most importantly, my journey to this point and why I was coming out now. Because I wanted people to understand me better, I talked about the pain I'd been through trying to hold this in and the impact that had on my mental health. After spending a lot of time getting dressed and hyping myself up, at 9:00 a.m. I hit Send. We were in virtual mode at the time, so I knew I'd have to show up on video as myself that day. This was one of the scariest moments of my life.

What came next shocked me. While sitting at my desk, questioning my life choices and what a fool I'd been, within five minutes I knew the answer to how people felt: I received over 250 emails with congratulations, warm welcomes, and so much more that day as the news spread. I also went on vacation for a week starting the next day because I knew I'd need some time off after the run-up to this announcement. My return to work was nerve-wracking, but people quickly adjusted to me.

My story centers on coming out at a major US corporation. However, many trans people go through this process at much smaller companies, such as in retail or service work. Smaller companies may have less robust inclusion efforts for marginalized communities, so your experience may differ from mine.

Your first step is to talk with any trans or nonbinary people who've already come out in your workplace, if any, so that you can get the lay of the land before proceeding. If this hasn't happened or you're unaware whether it has, I'd start by looking into your company's position on the LGBTQIA community. Go through the process to connect with HR so you have some protection.

I want to acknowledge that you only need to come out at work if you want to. Please do not feel that this is a requirement. If you decide you want to, you should review the topics below when you speak with HR:

1. If you're unaware, ask about LGBTQIA ERGs to see whether the community has an internal organization. Seek guidance from that group.
2. Start by coming out to HR and be clear and upfront.
3. Ask whether your workplace will support your coming out.
4. Determine whether your firm already has a guide for workplace transition. If so, ask for a copy and read it thoroughly. If not, HR will likely ask you to be a test case to build documentation.

5. With your HR rep, create a document with your plan to notify your coworkers of your change in gender. Include your boss in this conversation and planning process, with HR's help.
6. Write a letter, create a video, or plan an in-person event. A letter generally works best.
7. Prepare your materials and ensure your boss and HR rep see and are aware of the contents.
8. If possible, solicit support from someone higher up in the company than your boss. This person's job is to model acceptable behavior for the company. Work with HR and your boss to identify this person.
9. Pick a date to send your information to all applicable people. Many people pick a Friday afternoon and come to work as their authentic selves on Monday.
10. Document everything so that you have a paper trail if there are difficulties.
11. Discuss with your HR rep how people with adverse reactions will be handled.
12. Hope for the best, plan for the worst.

I'VE COME OUT, NOW WHAT?

Now that you've introduced people in your life to who you really are, we need to turn our attention to what comes next. Let's review what to consider as your various relationships move into the "getting to know you better" phase.

Partners

Figuring out what to do next depends on many factors. If the relationship can't work or your partner can't support you, you'll want to consider ending the relationship. If it went well or is a work-in-progress situation, read on.

More so than any other people in our lives, our partners must navigate their own type of transition as well as ours. They have to grapple with not only the idea of our being transgender or nonbinary but also their own identity with gender and sexuality, not to mention how their families will receive this news. They will likely feel many emotions even if they're supportive of us. They may still be dealing with anger, mistrust, betrayal, sadness, and more since you came out to them. They need grace and time like you did; you can't rush people through feelings.

I think a significant fear that most partners grapple with is the idea that being trans means you want to be with a different partner, such as assuming that all trans women will start dating men. This idea is driven in large part by the media portrayal of trans women and, frankly, the fact that society views any man who has feminine tendencies as an indication he's gay. This is a patently untrue narrative. This assumption is so ubiquitous that I don't know of any trans women who were in hetero-appearing relationships before transition and weren't asked whether they were gay instead. Many fears boil down to worry over loss of stability, safety, love, trust, or fidelity. Unless your partner was aware of the possibility that you're trans or nonbinary, your coming out is likely to be a huge surprise, as most of us keep this information buried quite deep down. While we know what's happening with ourselves, our partners may or may not see the signs and connect the dots to our being trans. It depends on how much they've observed and what we've let them see.

Some partners might have suspicions, and others may have no idea. Some partners do beautifully and travel with us through the process, some struggle but find their way through, some struggle and don't find their way through, and some will not move forward with us at all. These are all valid paths that the journey with your partner can take. To keep moving forward together, you'll need to keep some best practices in mind:

- Clearly communicate the pace at which you'd like to proceed and have those discussions. Everyone, including you, needs time to adapt. Ensure your partner knows what will happen and the timeline it will happen in. If your intention is for your partner to stay invested in the relationship, transparency will help significantly.
- When you share your transition plans, tell your partner what they should call you, what pronouns to use, how your presentation might change, and whether you're planning medical intervention with hormone therapy or various surgeries. Misleading them will make things even more difficult than being upfront.
- Ensure you each have people you trust to talk to, as some things need to be worked out with a nonjudgmental, neutral party.

- Be there for your partner and ask that they be there for you.
- Do not sacrifice your health for another person. If your mental, emotional, and physical health is at risk, be transparent and honest about that.
- Understand that even if your partner is entirely behind you, they will likely still have some difficulty as they watch you transform before their eyes. Change is hard for most people. While this process might be exciting and affirming for you, your partner may need time to adapt. If you intend for the relationship to survive, you must keep them informed and be open about your plans, which will require some discussion.
- Be prepared for your partner's friends and family to express opinions. Understand that your partner may get adverse reactions from their family and friends, which won't be helpful. Your partner will get almost as much flack as you do and will need your support to get through it.

Ultimately, healthy relationships fare better than others when it comes to difficulties. However, that comes down to each person being able to work through how they feel about something as deep-seated in their psyche as gender and sexuality.

Family & Friends

As with our partners, the aftermath of coming out can be tricky to navigate with friends and family. The best advice I have to give you is to be your authentic self with them as soon as they know. Why? Showing up after you come out gets people used to who you are and gets the ball rolling quickly.

When I came out to my circle of people, there were some I saw occasionally and some I saw weekly. The people I saw often adapted to me quickly, and the awkwardness passed swiftly. The people I saw less frequently generally took months to reach the same point, while some have never gotten there. Though this latter group used my name and pronouns with limited success, the stakes were low because we interacted only on the occasional phone call. However, I did not hold back on my presentation when I saw each person for the first time; I let them see the real me. For the most part, it made all the difference.

Tell your friends and family and then show yourself to them. Yes, it will feel awkward and scary for both of you, but that does pass quickly for those who truly accept you. As with partners, if your friends or family cannot and will not accept who you are, you do not owe them a relationship. Here are some tips to keep in mind:

1. You do not owe anybody the right to disagree with your transness.
2. Friends and family must work through their fears, which may take time. Ensure you care for yourself in these situations and set boundaries if needed.

3. In most cases, you'll be the first trans or nonbinary person they know. They're unprepared for this situation and likely have only misnomers, stereotypical information, or misunderstanding of the facts. In many cases, they have no idea how little they know. Again, if you plan to keep these people in your life, patience with their process of learning—as long as they *are* learning—may be required.

I recommend pointing this group of people to sources you trust on being trans or nonbinary, such as websites, books, and podcasts, so that you don't have to educate them all on every single detail.

Coworkers

Though we've covered coworkers a bit, there are some questions that need more specific attention. The workplace presents some unique challenges, so I want to answer some of the most common questions I've received.

How Will My Relationships with Coworkers Change?

Beyond the obvious changes in name, pronouns, and presentation, much more will change, particularly with how people relate to you at work and how you relate to them. Workplaces reinforce gender norms quite strongly. Hopefully you're welcomed and included by the other women or men in the office as applicable. Nonbinary people, however, tend to struggle a lot in this area because office mates want to categorize people into one of two groups, which may or may not work for you. All too often, nonbinary people are classified as "women lite" instead of being allowed to align themselves with groups they prefer. Oppositional sexism is at play for sure: if you're not 100 percent aligned with manhood, you get assigned to the women's side of affairs.

Your coworkers will interact with you in new ways. Still, you might be most surprised by your role in the office regarding the division of labor, expectations, opportunities, and the policing of your communication style. When everyone thought I was a man at work, for instance, my knowledge in an area of expertise was seldom questioned. Frankly, I received praise for my emotional intelligence, which was considered an incredible trait to have as a man in the corporate world. I cared deeply about my coworkers' well-being, which was considered out of the norm and a unique asset for a man to have. Rarely was I tasked with things like notetaking, even though I regularly volunteered for them. I was seen as weird for wanting to help with planning office events, judged whenever I was the one who stayed home with sick kids, and exaggeratedly praised for doing minor things in my kids' lives. I often heard I had the right amount of assertiveness and attention to detail as well as a soft touch that set my teams up for success. Every cisgender woman reading this is rolling her eyes by now.

Upon introducing the workplace to my true self, Erica, so much changed regarding the norms I was to follow. Within the first few weeks, some changes appeared in how people behaved around me, I was regularly asked to take notes for the team, my project decisions were questioned, and the knowledge I'd displayed for years was already fading in my coworker's eyes. I was assumed to know less than my direct reports and spoken over by most male colleagues. One manager told me I was being too direct and needed to use a more solicitous tone when checking on assignments I was overseeing, yet a few days later I heard I wasn't being assertive enough. I started getting sexist comments from male coworkers, and a superior chastised me for not joining the all-women planning team for an office event.

While I knew to expect all of this, my eyes opened when I started being included in the conversation with my female coworkers about far less savory behavior they'd been experiencing and then having similar experiences of my own. Again, I assumed some of this had been happening, but hearing and experiencing it across the board was wild. "Welcome to womanhood" was a phrase I often heard from my female coworkers, and my wife, when telling them what was happening to me.

Transmasculine people tend to have the opposite experience. They're suddenly seen as competent and are questioned and interrupted far less often. However, they also tend to find their support network vanish in favor of male corporate culture's lone-wolf work style. And of course, their transness can and likely will be used against them just as much as transwomen.

Indeed, my coming out at work wasn't all bad. I came to appreciate the circle of female camaraderie, and I got compliments on how I was showing up, how I handled people, and what I was wearing, including my makeup and my shoes. What I loved was the hype women gave each other. For years, I'd felt so alone as a man in the corporate world, but now I had people behind me and cheering me on.

Another thing I noticed was how recognizable I became at work. As you'll recall, I worked for a large bank with 50,000 employees across three continents, and my office was on the main campus in the Washington, DC, area. As I went about my day navigating meetings across three buildings, grabbing lunch on the campus, or attending large conference sessions, I was recognized everywhere. Despite my being in a prominent role, this was a new experience for me. I constantly heard comments and questions like, "Hey, you're Erica, right?" "Didn't I see you at a presentation for your division? I don't recall what, but I remember you, Erica!" and "Hey, it's good to see you again; remember we chatted in line for lunch a few months back?" On and on. People would look up and smile broadly or frown deeply. I'd get waves from people I was damn sure I'd never seen or met. And of course there were the stares; oh, those stares followed me everywhere.

Being trans or nonbinary in the workplace means you stand out everywhere. Your transness is perceived, and whether it's for good or for ill, it affects you constantly. Things will change in positive and negative ways.

Transition in the workplace is always an eye-opening experience that's never all roses for anyone who goes through it. Indeed, I had people change their opinion of me just because I was out as trans and no longer fit neatly into their worldview. I lost friends and supporters, and people on my team turned against me not because I was performing my job with less ability but because I dared to exist as myself in the workplace. Be prepared for things to change and get weird at work until you settle in and get used to how the workplace now views you.

As bad as all this sounds, I was happy to bring my whole self to work and get to know my peers without the mask I'd been wearing.

Do Transgender People Who Come Out at Work Go Through a Slump in Performance Reviews?

There seems to be little direct data on how trans and non-binary people do in performance reviews before and after transition. According to anecdotal information from the community, however, management perceiving a reduction in our performance post-transition is a common occurrence.

Many trans and nonbinary people report complex relationships with both their direct managers and their company policies. We experience a higher amount of anxiety, particularly because we face not only the same difficulties in the workplace that cisgender people do but also others' perceptions of our transgender status that add layers of unique problems. Furthermore, transgender people report higher rates of harassment of all kinds than cisgender people.

The reality is that most of the people we work with have done little, if anything, to assess their assumptions about the trans community. Many are working from "knowledge" gleaned in the more sensationalist media coverage of trans people, including in movies, talk shows, reality shows, and news segments, which rarely portray us in a positive light. When we factor in the community's political and religious points of view, at best we're misunderstood by people who are uneducated, and at worst people actively work against us in the workplace. So, soon after you come out at work, a negative review will likely occur in which it will be painfully obvious the rationale is rooted in public opinion and not in actual performance. This experience is so common that many trans people choose to start over at new companies after coming out to get a fair chance at being treated respectfully and receive recognition for their work.

So what do we do about it? Other than actually having effective inclusive workplace policies and education along with post-performance review auditing, we keep the receipts. A few guiding points on documenting your performance ahead of your next review are these:

1. Document every accolade, kudo, and celebratory comment you get on your performance, and reference it in reviews.
2. Benchmark your performance metrics before you transition in the workplace so you can compare them to the same metrics after you come out.
3. Keep thorough documentation of every negative interaction or comment you receive, especially if not tied to performance. You may need to show evidence of biased individuals.

4. Be on the record with HR about any difficult interactions with coworkers.
5. Understand that HR's prime responsibility is to protect the company from legal action, not to protect you. This changes when protecting themselves means protecting you.

All this being said, do transition at work, because showing up as your true self is worth it. Putting your authenticity on the table will make you a better employee, whether your coworkers see that or not. But always be prepared to move on and start over elsewhere as your whole self.

Should I Join an Employee Resource Group?

ERGs, also known as "employee resource groups," "affinity groups," or whatever your company might call them, are always worth looking into. They're a great source of information on all things LGBTQIA and typically have good programming to interact with. They're usually quite welcoming to the trans community, although I suppose there could be some that aren't. In my opinion, there are four main reasons you should look into them:

1. Depending on how you came to know you're trans or nonbinary, you may have yet to establish a community of peers. ERGs are a great place to make friends and broaden your network.
2. An ERG is a place to make your voice and experiences heard. Many companies look to their ERGs

for feedback on how they're doing, what initiatives to investigate, and how they can be better employers. An ERG is an excellent place to learn to use your voice and find the messages that are important to you.

3. Most ERGs have a year-round calendar of events, from acknowledging important days in the year to diving deep into various applicable topics to holding after-hours events. Some will bring speakers like me to talk about different perspectives. Consider working on some programming and being a speaker.

4. If you're with a more prominent company, you may have the chance to attend conferences centered on the LGBTQIA perspective.

Participating in an ERG is not required, but it's an excellent place to meet new people and expand your network.

Do I Need to Educate Everyone about Being Transgender Now That I'm Out?

You do not need to educate others!

I took the time to point people close to me to resources such as PFLAG and The Gender Dysphoria Bible so they could have a place to read up. However, I still received some questions from coworkers. You should not feel obligated to educate people, particularly if resources are available for them to review. People are endlessly curious, though, and all too often prefer that their education be served to them.

A way to approach this is to pick out a few resources you like and refer people to those as needed. I also recommend determining which topics you're willing to discuss and which you're not interested in discussing. Take note that you are only one person in the community, so before you choose to talk about an area of transness you're not experiencing, you should take the time to read up. People will ask you to speak for and justify the whole community when they know you're trans. Please feel free to say no whenever you want to. You do not owe anyone a discussion on transgender people.

You are not required to answer any question, certainly not if the person asking it is rude. Trans people are almost always served up as a salacious topic instead of a group of humans going about their day. Please know that you are *not* the ambassador for the trans community.

What Should I Consider When Searching for a New Job?

Job searching as an out trans person can be difficult. First, it can be hard to tell whether job rejection is because of anti-trans sentiments or a poor fit between your skills and the job. The reality is that without someone being explicit in their rejection, you'll likely never really know. The trans community at large is underemployed and underpaid, so it might be an experience you come across.

So what are we to do? Some people's approach has been to be upfront, while others don't broach the topic. I'm in the upfront category. You'll find it mentioned in my LinkedIn profile and resume for two reasons. The first is that I'm obviously a trans person on even the most casual inspection. The second and more important reason is that it allows me to interview recruiters about how LGBTQIA people are treated within the company I'm interviewing with. I choose to be upfront to make it clear who I am and what I will not tolerate. This way, there will hopefully be no surprises when I start a new job.

I can say that when I decided to move on from my last job, I found my current job relatively quickly, so my trans status didn't have an impact on me in this regard. It did allow me to understand how the company I now work for would support me. To be fully transparent with you, I work in tech, am a senior manager in my field, am sought after by companies that pursue DEI initiatives, and live in a major metropolitan area with plenty of roles I'd be interested in. My whole situation would be different if I lived in a small area with few roles applicable to me. I've also been there and done that even before I came out, and it was tough. Some factors are hard whether you're trans or not. However, I have trans and nonbinary friends who've struggled month after month to find a new role after being let go or laid off. Certainly, one of the reasons is the fact that they're transgender.

As with any job search, take the time to learn how your industry has changed terminology and requirements since your last foray into the market and understand jobs in your area. If possible, talk with people you know who work at the company you're applying to. Check in with a local LGBTQIA organization or the Human Rights Campaign to see whether the company has a rating with them. Any interview you take part in is also an opportunity to interview the interviewer and ask pertinent questions.

Finally, it's not a good idea to interview for a job as one gender but then show up as another on the first day of work. If you intend to work this job as your authentic self, then interview as your authentic self.

Chosen Family

Though rarely connected to us by blood, the people we choose to include in our circle of family are typically the ones who are most accepting of us. They're the ones who truly see us and celebrate who we are.

Why Should I Seek Out Chosen Family?

Over time, we form close bonds with people who don't have familial ties with us but become like our family. The queer community is full of people who might become closer to us than anyone else in life, and within it the concept of chosen family is prevalent. When the family in our lives rejects us, who better than those who share the same experiences to call family? These people accept us for who we are, affirm our authenticity, and can take the place of a sibling or parent. They are the family we choose.

Trans people in particular can have difficult family relationships, be it with parents or siblings who aren't affirming or with other close family who offer only negativity. I'm not saying you have to leave your family behind;

I am saying to add people to your life who can fill in the gaps others leave behind. In many cases, rejection isn't your fault because it takes someone refusing to acknowledge the truth of who you are, someone failing to see the person right in front of them, to force you out. The only way to prevent that is to give up what you know to be true and stuff yourself back into the closet. Who would tell a butterfly to go back to being a caterpillar? Family is meant to be a place of safety, acceptance, and love. Rejection has none of these qualities; it's based on an inability to work through prejudice and fear-based thinking. Family that rejects you would rather sacrifice you than work through their own shit.

While my wife is my best friend, lover, and the person I want to spend endless time with, and though I get on well with my family, these people cannot meet all my needs. No one person can hold all that you need in life. Indeed there are central figures, but you need to expand your circle. I have chosen family from the queer community, the trans community, and the cisgender heterosexual community. My wife has her own friends who are part of her chosen family. Together we have dear friends who are very much a part of our family.

The ultimate point is that your natal family may not be the only family you make or need. I'm certainly not saying blood family is lacking across the board. But you need more than these people can offer; you need a shared understanding.

What If I Have a Falling Out with a Chosen Family Member?

The commonalities or quirks of personality that pulled you together with someone can change or even sour over time. When friendships break up, especially close ones, that can be as difficult as family or even partner breakups. I've had a few harrowing experiences with these situations.

There are a few categories of breakups I've seen play out. The most common version is the slow fade, which is when you or your friend reaches out less or moves away or when life circumstances interfere. There are a lot of situations that fall under this umbrella. Sometimes life makes it hard for people to stay connected. Be patient and persistent in these situations. Eventually, it will either work out or you'll both realize it wasn't meant to last forever. Sometimes people simply come and go in our lives.

A less common but no less critical version of chosen family breakups is when you realize it's time to move on due to being at odds in some way that might have become clear to you recently. There will be people you meet who are trans, queer, or an ally that you eventually need to move on from. Just because someone is part of the community doesn't mean they share your viewpoint on everything. Situations appear when you realize a fundamental difference of opinion or more problematic behaviors cross your boundaries. For example, I've met trans people I thought I'd be close with only to find that they believe only certain people get to be trans, and only if they have the right surgeries, which goes against everything I'm about. I've been in situations with friends where they espoused racist beliefs, which is also not something I'm in any way about. For you, it could be something that seems benign, like a simple disagreement, but then spins way out of control.

At the end of the day, it might be that it's time for you to move on. You don't need to keep people in your life even if they were there for you in difficult times, especially if they no longer match up to who you are. Please try to have friends from many different walks of life so that you'll see more of life through others' eyes. Being exposed to diverse experiences leads to a life where you can be more empathetic, more understanding, and better able to support others.

I was once pretty close with someone in the LGBTQIA community, and it seemed like we would become tight, lifelong friends. I suggested to them that we work on a project together. While talking my way through my thought process, they told me we didn't feel the same way and then went off on me. To this day, I'm still unsure what went wrong. This person jettisoned me from their life for a rationale that did not ring true for me. I'm not everyone's cup of tea; I know there are areas of my life where I'm still growing and learning. But what they said didn't seem like the actual root of the problem. Though we could interact politely the few times we were in each other's orbit after this event, we never recovered. I was crushed and spent months working out how I felt about what had happened. I suspect my hurt at what felt like an attack by this person and my defense of myself fed into how they felt they could never really trust people.

I know this much: We all have hurts in our past and generational patterns at play in our everyday lives. Trans people are no different, and many of us are carrying extra layers of pain from living with the wrong gender for years. Give grace, but also know your boundaries.

CHAPTER 5

BEING

I chose "Being" as the name for this chapter because it deals with some advanced topics and issues that people living life as trans or nonbinary are likely to encounter as they go about their days out in the world. Life begins to slow down to some degree after all the changes that happen when we come out to our network, pick our name, change our wardrobe, and perhaps pursue medical intervention. As such, we come up for air and notice how we respond differently to our world.

While we will continue to evolve, most near-term changes happen in a relatively short time of 12–18 months. After this time, our mental bandwidth to look beyond our singular experiences increases, and we can see what others are going through as we become much more comfortable with ourselves. As a result, we may start dispensing advice to those who come after us, enter into public discourse, volunteer, or mentor others. During this period, we need to think about how we go through the world and the impact we have on it as people who represent the transgender community.

AM I THE ONLY TRANS PERSON PEOPLE KNOW?

Most likely, yes, you're the only trans person the people in your circle know. Hopefully you've begun to build a network of people who are also trans or nonbinary, whether online, in your community, at work, or through volunteer efforts you might have taken on. In the United States, there are about 1.6 million transgender people ages 13+, 1.3 million of which are 18 and older.[2] That's a small portion of society but still many individuals. While you hopefully know of many transgender people by now, most of America, and frankly most of every country, does not. This fact will become evident rather quickly. As I said in Chapter 4, most people aren't prepared for us and are unaware of how little factual information they know about the trans experience.

You're likely the first, the only, or one of the few trans or nonbinary people your circle of cisgender family, friends, and coworkers know. It's pretty startling to experience the deficit in practical knowledge most humans have. To them, you're going to be the person who represents the entirety of the trans community, and they'll assume your trans experience is the experience everyone has, which can feel like a heavy burden.

Why am I bringing this to your attention? Mostly to prepare you for how most people will react to you beyond the

---

2. Jody L. Herman, Andrew R. Flores, and Kathryn K. O'Neill, "How Many Adults and Youth Identify as Transgender in the United States?" UCLA School of Law William's Institute, June 2022, https://williamsinstitute.law.ucla.edu/publications/trans-adults-united-states/.

outright rudeness or hate we all expect. You're an ambassador whether you want to be or not. Does this mean you need to be everyone's educator? No. Does it mean you need to hold people's hands and help them feel comfortable with trans people? No. Does it mean you need to be the advocate in the room? No. However, it does mean people will want you to be and do all those things. If you take time to prepare for these situations, you'll be better able to handle them. Take the time to decide what you will and will not talk about. Determine how you will handle the situation when perceived as *the* trans person.

While hopefully well-intentioned, some people's natural curiosity may be wildly inappropriate. Though you know some people will be rude and you may be ready for it, what about people who have no idea they're being disrespectful? How will you handle those situations? Take the time to learn about the many different trans experiences. Determine what questions you will field and the ones you will not. Have an exit plan if you need one. Stay focused on your capacity and be true to that in public. You do not owe anyone an explanation, debate, or justification.

Remember, we are humans, not a flavor of bagel. Our existence is not up for debate. When you come across these people, know that no number of facts will sway them; they are not acting in good faith.

WILL I LOSE MY ANONYMITY?

Yes, you'll likely lose your anonymity in the transition process; it's a startlingly common experience. Many people I've known since coming out, myself included, live this fact daily. We're used to the idea that those of us who are visibly trans in public get curious looks. People stare and nudge their friends to draw attention to us, and some can be downright rude about it. However, what's shocking is when a stranger seems to know you. If you've experienced this, you know the disturbing feeling I'm talking about.

I'll give you an example to make this clearer. I recall walking into a coffee shop that had just opened near my office. I have a regular one that's closer, but I decided to give the new place a try. I ordered a caramel macchiato, my favorite, and gave my name when asked. I was busily responding to work messages on my phone and didn't interact with the barista after placing my order. Once my drink was ready, I grabbed it and left to head back to the office for a meeting. The coffee was great, by the way. It was a perfectly ordinary coffee shop interaction.

Here's where it gets weird. I returned to the new coffee shop four weeks later; I hadn't gone back since the first time, mostly because I'd forgotten about it since it was out of my way. When I walked in, the barista gave me a very excited, "Hi Erica! It's good to see you again!" I stopped dead in my tracks 6 feet from the counter, very confused about why this person knew me and I didn't know them. I could only assume they were the person who took my order the last time. This interaction freaked me out, and I mishandled the situation because I was so surprised. While most people might be pleased that a barista knew their name, I knew this was something more. I was notable and worth recalling as "the trans lady named Erica." Granted, coffee shops are queer bastions, but this local shop certainly did not read as one, nor did the barista.

This situation happens often at any place I frequent more than once. I've had waiters recall me from two months prior, store owners recognize me from returning an item, and cashiers at grocery stores whose line I'd been in one time recall my last visit. This has even happened with people on the street I've walked past who've given me a familiar wave many weeks after the first time I'd seen them. At this point in my life, I'm so used to this fact that it no longer phases me.

As members of the trans community, we stand out, and we become recognizable because we're different from the rest of the crowd. I've talked to at least 20 trans and nonbinary people with the same stories. Know that it's likely to happen, take extra safety precautions, and you might even learn to throw an uninviting face at someone when necessary. When they're overly conspicuous in their acknowledgment, cisgender people have little understanding of the amount of attention they draw to us from everyone else nearby. And it can certainly feel like they've placed a target on our back, no matter their intentions. Maybe once society is much more comfortable with trans people, we'll be able to pass unnoticed.

WHY DO PEOPLE FEEL ENTITLED TO TALK ABOUT MY TRANSNESS?

The root cause of people talking about our transness is that many feel we owe them something just for existing as trans near them. It's a controversial view, indeed, but hear me out and decide for yourself. What drives this home for me is that when we place those outside of the trans community into three groups, we can see they all want one essential thing: for us to share their point of view in order to validate them. We're something they feel ownership of.

First are the people who think it's their job to pass judgment on us, second are those who want us to satiate their curiosity, and third are those I think of as entry-level allies who want our approval to validate their "good deeds." There are certainly other groups I'm leaving out, such as actual allies, but I'm talking about the people who see us as a talking point instead of a person.

What blows my mind daily is the people who think it's their job to tell us we're wrong for being trans or nonbinary. Having a stranger come up to me in person or online and start in on the fact that my existence is up for debate and should be stopped and legislated out of existence is an incredibly wild take. In what world does a person think they have the right to tell anyone who they should be, let alone a stranger? They don't know me, my life, or my situation, and who I am has absolutely no impact on them, yet they feel the need to tell me who they think I am.

The root of this problem is that these people believe the world must conform to their limited points of view; otherwise, they feel out of control, invalidated, and like they've lost whatever power they think they've taken from others. Effectively, these people have a zero-sum-game mindset, believing that being wrong means they lost something, yet it was never theirs in the first place. For these people, anti-trans rhetoric is their whole deal, and they very likely hold bigoted views in a lot of areas of their lives. These are people looking for a problem to give them meaning instead of looking for what's meaningful in their own lives. We are the problem that gives them meaning, so if they can't silence us, they have nothing valuable in life.

Curious people tend to exercise the human trait of centering themselves over those they pester. They put zero thought into whether the information they seek is meaningful, and they choose to forgo educating themselves, instead badgering marginalized communities for education. People in this group aren't just asking annoying questions to the trans community; they're asking questions about everything around them to everyone around them. Their curiosity doesn't run deep enough for them to consider self-education important, so they believe other people should do their work for them. This group consists of those who get offended when you refuse to answer their questions, no matter how politely you do it. They cause harm because their curiosity is insensitive, thoughtless, and something they feel we owe them. We are their curiosity of the moment.

The third group is something different. These people think they're allies, but either they're only tolerant and can't tell the difference or they haven't done the work to be a true ally. At heart they are virtue signalers; they'll come up to us and find a way to be loud about their support of us in a performative way, though they don't know this is what they're doing. On many occasions and in many public settings, this group has brought me to the attention of everyone. I've had them be way too comfortable with my body, and many have spoken over and for me instead of allowing me to speak capably for myself. People in this group treat me like they own my transness; they act like it serves them and not me. Granted, I know their intentions are good, though incredibly ill-informed. More so than the others, this group does damage by making us a target in public settings, spreading misinformation, and generally alienating the trans community they think they're an ally of. They do more harm than the other two groups combined, mainly because they need our validation of their good deeds as allies. I find them prickly. They're easily insulted at the most basic redirection, and their "allyship" gets revoked based on our relative likability at the moment, as if they're removing something of tremendous value.

There's a yoga class my wife and I go to occasionally. A few times, a cisgender lady joined the class and made a point to acknowledge me and be friendly, but she entirely ignored my wife, who was standing next to me, and she interrupted her to draw my attention. We saw her out and about once, and when she came up to me to say hello and mentioned yoga class, I pointed out my wife to her again. She continued to ignore my wife. At the next class, she again spoke to me and ignored my wife despite the fact that the two of us were chatting when she came up and interrupted. I'm the only trans person in this class, and my status is in no way a secret. This is purely the virtue signaler in action: she wants me to see her allyship more than she wants to acknowledge who I am—and the disruption she's causing every time. It's rude to me and incredibly dismissive to my wife, who *is* my greatest ally.

Unfortunately, I have quite a few stories precisely like this one. These people don't want to engage with our humanity; they want a pat on the back.

ARE ALL TRANSGENDER PEOPLE THE SAME?

I really shouldn't have to say this, but transgender people are not a monolith. Whether you're trans, an ally, or a friend, family member, or coworker, you need to think about trans people as coming from many points of view instead of a singular one. My experience and my choices in my expression are unique to me. We've hit on this topic in various ways, but I want to drive this home.

Being transgender spans all categories of people regardless of nationality, sex assigned at birth, age, race, education, socioeconomic status, and any other dimension you can apply. As such, there are millions of trans and nonbinary people globally. Exact statistics are difficult to come by, as definitions of what it means to be transgender differ across the globe. Many people fear participating in polls due to continuing discrimination, and efforts are still being made to include such statistics in global census data. However, one survey conducted in 2022 found that 1 percent of the global population describes themselves as transgender; 1 percent as nonbinary, gender nonconforming, or gender fluid; and 1 percent as neither but different from male or female.[3] That equates to about 81 million people in each group. No matter how you look at it, millions of people certainly isn't an anomaly as some would

---

3. Ipsos Group S.A., *LGBT+ Pride 2023: A 30-Country Ipsos Global Advisor Survey* (Paris, France: Ipsos, 2023), https://www.ipsos.com/sites/default/files/ct/news/documents/2023-05/Ipsos%20LGBT%2B%20Pride%202023%20Global%20Survey%20Report%20-%20rev.pdf.

have us believe. We must start learning some nuance when considering groups of this size.

When we speak about the community, we must acknowledge the incredible diversity within its confines. Do not make assumptions, do not apply your experience to all people, and do not forget the outsized impact of socioeconomic standing and country of origin. We also have to remember that the most socially acceptable portion of the community is White trans women. When we focus solely on their experience, we erase the experience of so many others. Trans women don't all have bottom surgery, some trans men menstruate, and nonbinary people may choose medical intervention or not. The trans community is vast, vibrant, and full of wonderful representation. Referring to us collectively by using only information on a subgroup is shortchanging everyone else.

I am representative of some trans women, not *the* representative of all trans people. Before you speak about trans experiences at large, you need to take the time to understand the intersectionality of the community. And if transgender people are being spoken for in a room where there are no trans people, stop what you're doing until trans people share that space with you, especially if you're an ally.

WHO SHOULD I HAVE IN MY TRANS NETWORK?

Though the question of who we should have in our trans network could've been in Chapter 4 about relating, it makes more sense here because a network takes time to build up,

and the type of people in your network may serve other pur-
poses than solely being friends. The purpose of a network
is to build connections with people from various walks of
life, those who help expand our experiences, understanding,
and information-sharing ability. I'm talking about trans and
queer people in the workplace and in our industries as well
as people who work in advocacy for marginalized communities, local and national government functions, social services,
the military, medical and legal professionals, and the media.
Frankly, I have yet to come across an industry where there is
no LGBTQIA representation.

I have connections in all the areas I just listed. Why should
you? Because it means you have exposure to a wealth of information and a variety of perspectives, which gives you a much
more contextualized understanding of the state of trans and
nonbinary people. Hearing various voices from across the
breadth of the trans and nonbinary community is essential.
Furthermore, it gets you closer to making a connection with
someone who has an experience like yours if you need guidance.

Your network is essential because the trans community is
a small portion of the people represented within your country.
We need to see ourselves in others. We must hold the trans
family together by continuing to develop an interconnected
network to spread information effectively. This action is rooted
in self- and community preservation. These connections also
allow us to act collectively, to show up in mass, and to stand
up for the rights of trans people more effectively.

You can find these people on professional platforms such
as LinkedIn and social media platforms such as Instagram,
TikTok, and Threads. Please stay off X (formerly Twitter), as

that platform is a toxic hellscape for trans people. There are organizations worth following as well. Please see the Reader Resources section at the end of this book for more information.

SHOULD I TELL MY FRIEND WHO'S QUESTIONING THEIR GENDER THAT THEY'RE TRANS?

The trans community refers to people who haven't transitioned or come out and may not be at the point in their lives where they're ready to deal with the possibility of being transgender as "eggs," a direct reference to a chick waiting to hatch and blossom into their authentic self. Every trans person is an egg at some point.

Sometimes when we come across eggs, we're aware that they may be trans before they are. Other times we want them to transition before they're ready. Your inclination might be to help them avoid some of the pain you've been through yourself. However, the prime directive of the trans community is that we don't crack eggs; we don't tell people who they are or when it's time to come out.

The reality is that you can't make someone be ready any sooner than they would be on their own. Coming to know you're trans is a complicated and life-altering process. Rushing someone through the crucial sorting-it-out period will do them far more harm than allowing them to be where they are. No matter how sure you are or how good you think it will be for them, when you put your priorities ahead of theirs, you force the issue. We all get it, and we've all been there. But pushing eggs forward is a mistake that can have disastrous consequences for them while you'll have none. Please check yourself if you're considering cracking an egg.

Frequently, people who have yet to transition seek out others who've already done so to confirm their feelings one way or the other or to get a sense of what's coming their way. They may also seek out confidants who aren't trans, and the same rules apply. No matter what they say, they're not asking you to force their hand or to take away their agency. They must entirely own this highly personal decision, which takes courage, conviction, and resiliency. When you steal that from them by forcing their hand or outing them to make them move forward, it goes badly far too often.

Our job is not to propel eggs forward but to be a sounding board for them, providing information that may help them feel safe enough to take the next steps.

WHAT IF I THINK SOMEONE ISN'T TRANS ENOUGH?

I've touched on this topic twice so far, but I want to address it head-on here. I'm going to be incredibly blunt, so consider this a fair warning.

You have no business judging other people's transness. You are not them, you have not walked in their shoes, and you have nothing but your judgment as a reference point. If you're enforcing rules for transness, you need to take a step back. Whether that be surgeries you think people must have, what their presentation must look like, or beliefs you feel must be true for someone to be valid as a trans person, you've gone down the wrong path. It's bullshit. It's trans erasure from inside our community, and it's incredibly harmful and elitist.

Perhaps you're unsure exactly what I'm getting at, so I'll paint you a picture: A high-fem trans woman tells you you're not trans *unless* you've had bottom surgery, top surgery, and a variety of other cosmetic procedures. She insists your dysphoria must be severe and your presentation must be ultra masc or ultra fem, she typically comes out hard against those who aren't dating people of the opposite gender, and she denies the existence of nonbinary people altogether. These people are out there.

Frankly, these stipulations are absolute deal-breakers. You must walk away if you encounter someone espousing any of them, let alone multiple. These are the extremists of the community. I want to be clear that while this makes them truly awful people, it does not invalidate their transness. Narcissism is not mutually exclusive with being transgender.

If you hold these beliefs, you need to reevaluate why you feel you need to control the trans community and ask yourself how you're any better than the anti-trans community. The harm done by these beliefs is genuinely horrible, which is why people who hold them are referred to by the trans community as "transmedicalists" or "truscum." They force many people back into the closet for months or years and tragically leave some feeling they have no option left but to unalive themselves.

SHOULD I CONSIDER BEING A BIG SISTER OR BROTHER?

Yes, you should absolutely consider becoming a big sister or brother! I love being a big sister to my trans and nonbinary siblings, and I highly recommend it if you have the capacity and patience to meet people where they are. It's very much a tradition for a member of the trans community to take someone coming into their transness under their wing. Our lived experiences are invaluable assets for anyone who's just figuring things out. And it can be pretty rewarding to watch someone blossom.

The value of being a big sibling is twofold. First, as you've likely experienced yourself, it's lonely when you first get started because most of us don't have a trans friend or family member to talk to. By connecting with you as their trans elder, your little sibling could find invaluable insight. This is particularly true because so much of our community exists online, which is often impersonal and contains questionable advice. If someone asks if they can connect you with their friend or family member who just came out, say yes. Second, your little sibling can feel validated, air out their fears with someone who's lived the experience, and hopefully gain confidence to move forward. You can also bring them into the community, connect them to others, teach them the norms, and help set them up for success.

One of my favorite moments is when my little siblings support a younger sibling by paying it forward. However, there are a few things we need to review:

1. We do not crack eggs.
2. We do not take care of people; they need to find their own way forward with some gentle guidance, not have you make all their decisions for them.
3. Be sure you have the mental and emotional capacity. Taking on a sibling means you need to show up for them. Rather than being at their beck and call, make yourself available to chat when it works for both of you.
4. Many are in a fragile state at first, so be gentle and considerate. They will likely also make mistakes with you as they find their way; when this happens, redirect them and explain why.
5. Set boundaries! You determine what information you want to reveal about yourself, how invested you become, and what the deal-breakers are in this relationship.
6. If they aren't a good fit for you, try to send them to someone who is.
7. Please do not keep them to yourself; introduce them to others.
8. Please encourage them to fly, not stay in the nest with you. You don't want your baby birds to imprint on you and not explore the world.
9. Know when you're in over your head, and send them to their therapist or doctor.
10. Pass on as much information as possible, and point to reliable sources when you can.

Being a big sibling can be incredibly rewarding. As with any relationship, though, it needs to work for both of you.

And it should support the idea that your new sibling will take off on their own someday.

IS IT OKAY NOT TO KEEP UP WITH ALL THE NEGATIVE MEDIA ABOUT TRANS PEOPLE?

It's absolutely okay not to keep up with negative media. I regularly take breaks from social media, the news cycle, and the legislative state of affairs of LGBTQIA people. At a certain point, all the negativity you consume online, which adds to what may be going on in your life, can be overwhelming. No matter the external source of distress, you must regularly take breaks and spend time with yourself and those you love.

During Pride 2023, I worked a stressful tech job, planned some of my company's activations, and participated in activations for other companies. Thoughtless collaborations with the LGBTQIA community between two huge global name-brand companies brought America to a boiling point, with the conservative half of the country boycotting both brands. The legislative state of affairs was also at one of its worst points with hundreds of anti-trans bills making their way across the country. Pride felt heavy to a lot of people. I put a lot into the event and planned to use it as a launching pad to progress my speaking career. I came out of that month incredibly drained, as did several of my friends who are public speakers. Afterward, I took some time off because I felt hopeless about the work we were all doing. Initially I planned to take a week off, which stretched into two weeks, then a month, then several months. My plans for this period fell apart, and I lost all momentum. It was October before I felt inspired to get back to work. There are so many people involved in the larger trans community that were exhausted by the end of Pride 2023. Frankly, I almost gave up participating completely, and some still wrestle with doing so.

No matter your level of community engagement or how much anti-trans rhetoric you come across, you need to find the time to pull back, reflect, and recharge. I spent time with queer friends and my inner circle of friends and family, limited my social media consumption, and did things that brought me happiness.

You must find ways to recharge your batteries and invest in trans joy. Trans joy is the experience of feeling gender euphoria, which is found in the clothes you wear, self-care, being with other trans people, or doing an activity typically aligned with your true gender, for example. Effectively, it means doing what makes you feel most at home and aligned with your authentic self. I'm a big fan of finding joy in life in general, but for trans and nonbinary people it's much more critical. I take joy in the success and celebratory moments of my trans siblings, in wearing my favorite outfit, in being with queer people, and in a hundred other little things like getting my nails done. I stop and acknowledge these moments for a few reasons:

1. It feels good and soothes my soul.
2. It becomes all too easy to get bogged down in the hostile forces of anti-trans people, and having a hit of joy helps me maintain a healthy state of mind.

3. When others experience my joy, it normalizes my existence as trans as a good thing. Because of this, I share joy with as many people as possible.
4. I do what I can to join people in their joy so that it spreads.

When we focus on joy, we reinforce that our love for ourselves is more important than what anyone else has to say about our transness. It helps break the negative feedback loop. My joy allows me to constantly remind myself that the love I hold for who I am as a trans woman is far greater than the hate sent my way from anti-trans individuals. As such, their negativity has far less of an effect on me. This helps me stay focused on what I'm doing while wading through the muck out there. This act of incredible self-love I've given myself by transitioning is also my most significant tool in showing people that trans and nonbinary folk are a vital and vibrant part of society. After all, it's tough to demonize a group of individuals and make it stick when that same group takes joy in its very existence. It's far easier to hate the idea of someone than to hate a person who's joyfully existing in the world.

So yes, take breaks, and take the time to invest in yourself and your mental health so that you can come back and continue to navigate how hard the world can be for transgender people.

CHAPTER 6

ADVOCACY

In this final chapter, I want to focus on some of the questions that come my way regarding advocacy. First, I want you to know that getting involved in advocacy work is not a requirement, nor does it make you a better trans or nonbinary person than others. Yet, I do encourage you to support our larger community in advocacy if possible.

Advocacy takes passion, conviction, and a willingness to listen and learn. Your most powerful tool will be in learning about and understanding intersectionality because so many people in the LGBTQIA community are marginalized in multiple ways. To uplift trans experiences, you must start with BIPOC, in particular Black trans experiences. Until the most marginalized among us can step forward, none of us can. Each of us needs to understand the impact of various dimensions of diversity, including gender, sexuality, education, housing status, relative wealth, location, and more. Do you need to spend a bunch of time reading before getting involved? No, but you should be working to increase your knowledge.

On that note, being trans and nonbinary does not grant you an antibias point of view. You may have unresolved internalized racism, sexism, or ableism that needs investigation. You must learn to recognize your biases and work to remove them. The Wheel of Privilege and Power, a resource I've linked to in the Reader Resources section, is a great place to start recognizing and understanding your privilege.

I've had the honor of serving on the board of a transgender nonprofit and have held various positions within chapter and national ERGs for major corporations. While I've been fortunate to attend conferences focused on LGBTQIA people in the workplace, participate in panel discussions, plan engagements, and liaise between the trans community and the workplace, there is one thing I enjoy the most: meeting people. I love it when I have the chance to meet and connect with someone new in my workplace and bring advocacy and support to them. It makes my day. My heart is in individual interactions and celebrating our authenticity together.

I also had the opportunity to create a monthly podcast at one of my previous companies. I brought on an associate each month to talk about their life, job, family, and queerness both in and out of the workplace. Helping people tell their stories to a broad audience, especially in a way that normalizes the LGBTQIA community to the cisgender heterosexual community, is one of my proudest achievements.

WHERE DO I GET STARTED IN ADVOCACY?

If you're interested in getting started in advocacy, that makes me so happy. Please know that it will require you to learn from others, so you'll need to be willing to listen to people who've been doing this work longer than you have. I typically point people down two paths to explore in unison: (1) encouraging people to learn more about the transgender and larger LGBTQIA community, and (2) researching organizations in your area that need volunteers.

There is much to learn about the community, but a few essential areas will give you grounding. While the following list points you in the right direction, I'll leave you to read up on these topics instead of hand-feeding you the information. Self-education is an important skill to have in general, but it's vital in the world of advocacy:

- Read up on the history of Pride and the Stonewall Riots. The information you'll gain there directly relates because while Pride is a month-long celebration, it's still a protest today. A central figure in that event is Marsha P. Johnson, who is central to both Pride and the trans community.
- The Gay and Lesbian Alliance Against Defamation (GLAAD) has an LGBTQIA Community Calendar with many significant days of recognition, and reviewing and reading up on them at glaad.org/reference/calendar/ is worth your time. They cover every letter in the LGBTQIA acronym, from Pride to Asexual

Awareness Day. It's an excellent resource for getting familiar with all the important days of the year.

- Read up on trans history. You might start with how different cultures have recognized more than just male and female genders. The Hijras of Thailand and India and the Indigenous people of North America are just two groups of many that are worth reading about.

- The Hirschfeld Institute for Sexual Research in Berlin is another critical topic in trans history. It not only represents the first-known modern-era trans clinic but was the first institution targeted in the Holocaust; it was raided on May 6, 1933, and burned down four days later. Dora Richter was a patient of the Hirschfeld Institute and is likely the first trans woman to receive gender-affirming surgery in 1931.

- In 1952, celebrity Christeen Jorgensen became the first trans person widely known to receive gender-affirming surgery.

- There have been a host of important trans people over the last 60–70 years who are worth spending your time learning about.

- Read up on Transgender Day of Remembrance.

- Look into the significance of ball culture.

- Understand transgender portrayal in the media and how it has evolved over the last 50 years.

- Read up on broader topics such as anti-racism, feminism, intersectionality, and DEI efforts.

The other track I mentioned is investigating local organizations or activities in your area to participate in:

- Volunteer with your local Pride festival.
- Join LGBTQIA support groups.
- Support local shelters.
- Join the closest chapter of a nationwide organization, such as the Human Rights Campaign or PFLAG.
- Call your elected officials and make your support known.
- Sign petitions and attend protests and/or demonstrations.
- Advocate at the local school level to ensure trans youth are treated fairly.
- Vote and pay attention to electoral races at the local level.
- Center intersectionality and diversity in your efforts.

WHAT SHOULD I KNOW ABOUT GETTING INTO ADVOCACY AND ALLYSHIP AS SOMEONE WHO ISN'T TRANS?

The question of whether a non-trans person should get involved in trans advocacy typically comes from people who have a trans person in their lives. You might be a parent of a trans child or sibling, maybe you're a close friend of someone who's trans, or perhaps you fully support trans people and want to be involved in efforts to move us forward in society. To that end, I want to bring three topics to your attention.

First, having a trans person in your life does not automatically make you an expert or well-informed on the topic; it does mean you have a point of reference, though. Far too often, those who haven't read up on trans and nonbinary people rely on knowledge that's very specific to a singular trans person

ADVICE FROM YOUR TRANS AUNTY

and may erroneously believe all people in the community are just like them. While you can certainly advocate for the trans person in your life, you still need to learn deeply about the topic to support the whole community. More than once I've come across a trans ally whose allyship was entirely rooted in the person they knew, leveraging that specific person's experience in an attempt to shut down the broad spectrum of trans people because they assumed everyone was just like their friend. Efforts led by people in this category fall far short and typically alienate far more people than they support. Reading this book should be opening your eyes to this fact.

You can support the person close to you in advocacy efforts, but you'll be most effective once your education is self-driven and not reliant on that one person. I recall coming across a situation like this on social media. A close friend of a trans woman was highly critical of other trans women because they weren't like her friend. She kept referencing behaviors her friend exhibited, such as being attracted to cis men, and insisted this was true for all "real" trans women. By the time this gal deleted this particular post, she had more than 1,500 replies from trans people calling out how wrong she was.

The second item to consider is knowing your place in a discussion about transgender people. While I love a passionate ally, their lack of lived experience as a trans person means they need to center on people who do have lived experience. Remember, your voice should support ours, not be louder than ours. Do not derail the discussion or center it on yourself. I'm not saying you don't have a valuable opinion or voice; I'm saying you shouldn't speak over my voice as a trans person. I recall being at an LGBTQIA-centric conference a few years ago where an ally made an unfortunate comment out of ignorance. The other allies in the room spent so much time shouting at this person and shutting them down that none of the trans community members could make themselves heard. They were so focused on this person that those of us to whom the comment was directed couldn't speak.

Speaking from the trans experience is more important than discussing it as an ally. Furthermore, when people with multiple marginalizations are the topic, you need to support the conversation rather than put yourself at the center of it. For instance, a White trans woman should support the experience of a Black trans woman before her own.

Third and finally, understand that allyship is personal. By that I mean what I need in an ally may be different from what my friend or my community needs in an ally. It's always good practice to check in with the people around you as you get to know them to see what they need from you in allyship. For example, if my wife takes the lead in introducing us to other people, she refers to me as her wife Erica and finds a way to use my pronouns. This sets the tone and results in most people following her lead. She simply says, "I'm Melissa, and this is my wife, Erica. Nice to meet you." We check in with each other about whether I'll address my trans status with someone new, and she'll let me know if a public bathroom seems safe for me to use, not to mention the other hundred ways she acts as my ally.

These are just a few examples, and the more you know someone, the more you can specifically be their ally. Take the time to ask what they might need from you.

HOW CAN I RECOGNIZE MY RELATIVE POSITION TO OTHER MARGINALIZED PEOPLE?

It's crucial to understand intersectionality and how people can be part of multiple marginalized communities. Though I've mentioned this before, I want to talk about accounting for situations when you may have more privilege than others in the community.

I understand the queer experience, the trans experience, the trans woman experience, and more, but all of those have been rooted in my experience as someone who's White. No matter how hard my life is, the world is more accessible to me than to those who have more multiplicities of marginalization. Moving into the advocacy space means learning about experiences beyond our own and respecting others when our relative privilege is higher.

To provide some clarity, if you're a White trans woman, regardless of whether you've known since childhood or only figured it out more recently, you still have more privilege in play than most people. This concept applies if you're not BIPOC or have fewer lived experiences with people perceiving you as female compared to other women. To be clear here, I am not in any way implying you are not discriminated against, nor am I denying that you experience prejudice or even oppression. What I am saying is to show respect to those who have experienced these facts of life longer and in more ways than you have. Queer Black women have experienced an entirely different level of discrimination, prejudice, and oppression than you have.

I'm a White queer trans woman who is well-paid in the high-tech field and lives in a liberal-leaning city in the metro area of Washington, DC, with access to an excellent trans clinic and specialists. I hold a Master of Science in Business Leadership and Management, am able-bodied and neurotypical, and have citizenship status in the United States. While I've experienced real hardship in my life, marginalization was never a factor until after I transitioned. My life differs from that of many people I'm involved with in advocacy. While anti-trans rhetoric, laws, and misogyny do have an impact on me, my lived experience is that I've lost little privilege since transition because of the factors I mentioned. That's not true for everyone, but it is for me. So when I enter advocacy spaces, I carry that knowledge with me and work to lend my privilege where possible. And I ensure that my experience doesn't overtake the voices in the room with decidedly less privilege than me.

Remember, BIPOC people have experienced oppression in every way possible for centuries. And women have struggled to gain the right to vote, own land, and have a bank account in their name, and now they're fighting for reproductive freedom—again. You may be able-bodied and have no idea how hard the world is for those who are not. Your experience may or may not include multiple marginalizations, and you need to be aware of the context others have that you may not.

Please take the time to explore your privilege, to understand how it does and does not relate to others, and to make space for those with more lived experience than you because they've been living with this shit for far longer. Again, your experience isn't less valid, you just need to understand its context compared to others.

HOW DO I FIND MY VOICE IN ADVOCACY SPACES?

Finding your voice is an incredibly personal journey, and my guidance is more about what to think about than what to do. You can certainly improve how you speak and write, and figuring out your message is the most critical step. As such, an important aspect is being knowledgeable and well-read about your topic. Let's jump into a recommended thought process, assuming you've already done the work to educate yourself.

1. **Determine what you're passionate about.**

   If you're reading this book, then it's safe to assume trans advocacy is a point of focus for you. However, I urge you not to focus your voice on *all* facets of being transgender but on one aspect that draws out passion in you. There are two reasons for this: (1) people respond when the message feels alive, and (2) being a transgender generalist requires a lot of learning and may be too broad a path when you're starting out. Pick a specific trans topic such as news, the legal state of affairs, medical information, culture, or presentation, for example. Whatever you choose should feel authentic, as people respond better when they see the real you.

2. **Get comfortable.**

   Know your topic well, and take time to practice speaking and writing about it. The more you do, the more relaxed you'll become. And in that comfort, your audience will build trust in you. It also means you can handle questions that come your way with grace. And believe me, questions will come your way, and this is when most people fall apart. If you cannot field questions and give thoughtful answers, you will get picked apart. Practice with people you trust. Have them ask you questions, then ask for their honest feedback. The more feedback you get, the better aligned your message will become.

3. **Develop your sound.**

   Record and then listen to yourself speak. Are you going too fast, speaking too softly, or halting in your delivery? Are you concise or lengthy? Does the thread get lost? This comes from practical experience, and recording yourself is a great way to start.

4. **Put it all together and brace for impact.**

   Once you feel your message is clear, you have to get out there and see what happens. Be prepared to miss the mark, be open to making changes, and apologize if you make a misstep. You're not always going to get it right, especially in the beginning, so you need to have tough skin and a willingness to get back out there. Hopefully you hit home with a talking point. If this happens on social media, you'll receive negative comments, which leads me to my next point.

5. **Ignore the hate.**

   Hate will come your way, and people might say awful things in response to you when they disagree. Do not let their hate own you, and do not waste your time taking their bait. They'll try to pull you off the message and never act in good faith. Your message is not for these people. It's vital to develop a thick skin and the ability not to take in what others say about you because it's meant only to tear you down.

I've been public speaking for most of my career in design and technology. I'm used to getting up in front of people to discuss the various initiatives I'm leading. I've spoken at conferences, on panels, and led workshops. The times I was most successful were the times I knew my topic well and could talk about it sincerely. Yes, I got nervous every time, but my nerves passed as I'd begin my talk. The nerves were tough to deal with at first, but I eventually learned to recognize them as my body getting ready to do my thing. When I can engage with the audience, I do my best work because we all have a discussion together instead of me presenting a lecture. Learning that I do best when I have feedback from the audience was a game changer, and I quickly became a better speaker after that realization.

Think back to a conversation or talk you gave that went well. What was it that made it work for you? Figuring that out will move you to the next level fast.

WHAT CAN WE DO TO IMPROVE ALLYSHIP?

Despite what you might think, there are many good allies to the trans community. Still, many have work to do to improve.

Allies should take ownership of their own education, yet in my experience, many consume the wrong information or need help grasping the content correctly. For allies reading this book and those interested in working with allies, I suggest the following: look at different groups of potential allies people belong to so that you know what you're working with and can point them towards the next step.

In my time, I've come across six distinct groups of people:

1. Anti-trans
2. Indifferent
3. Tolerant
4. Nascent ally
5. Ally
6. Developed ally

The anti-trans group actively works against trans people. Through their bigotry, people in this group demonize us, create anti-trans laws, commit hate acts, and work to undermine us in any way they can. No amount of talk or education will change this group's mind, and as long as they belong to this group, no amount of talk or education will convert them to allies.

The indifferent group, while not actively hating the trans community, isn't interested in supporting us either. People in this group frequently work from a biased point of view, usually because they know nothing better. They may progress in time, but it's unlikely they could ever become an ally, at least not until something causes them to develop some tact.

People in the tolerant group think of themselves as allies, but in reality they aren't. They believe their "acceptance of our existence" is a favor and that they've done all they need to do. They won't take action against us but likely won't do much to help us either. They can certainly advance to true allyship but need education on transgender people to get there.

Those in the nascent ally group have set their feet on the path but are likely working on assumptions rather than education. They feel positive about us but are either unsure how to improve or unaware they need to improve. This is the group most people get frustrated with when they say allies are terrible. Those in this group are well-intentioned but genuinely aren't informed enough to understand how their actions can cause problems for the trans community. Education and time spent listening to trans experiences would do wonders for this group.

The ally group consists of those who've had some education and know what to do and say and what not to do and say. They're willing to hear where they still have work to do, and they will stand with and support us. They've come a long way but may lack nuance, depth, and perhaps experience in knowing trans people well. Working to gain context and application of their allyship will move them to the final group.

The developed ally group is very knowledgeable and actively advocates along with us. These people know when to speak and when to listen, and they show up for us on the front lines. They've spent time learning about trans lives, they understand intersectionality, and they have the courage and conviction to stand up for us. Developed allies can be counted on to do the work and to show up with us, and they're the people all allies should aim to emulate.

So how do we move people through these groups? First and foremost, it starts with the individual taking the time to educate themselves. Unfortunately, many people don't know this is the first significant step and believe their acceptance is all the trans and nonbinary community needs. While that support is wonderful to have, trans people must also have active allies on our side to change the tide of anti-trans rhetoric because there are just too few of us. If you have the bandwidth, particularly as a developed trans ally, let people know educating themselves is where their focus should be. If you have a trans person in your life and want to be a good ally, do the work to learn, show up for them, and spread the word to the people you know. Be the example for other allies to follow.

WHAT DOES ADVOCACY IN THE WORKPLACE LOOK LIKE?

Marginalized communities need more advocacy in the workplace. Unfortunately, less than half of Fortune 500 companies released diversity disclosures in 2023, and there's still a long way to go. DEI goals can undoubtedly be pursued in any company, whether it has 50 employees or 100,000 and whether its focus is pay equity, diverse hiring, or acknowledging and helping educate employees on various days of note in the calendar. These are all goals worth striving for.

At medium to large corporations, for example, it's common to see efforts include ERGs that are aligned to the LGBTQIA community and many other marginalized groups. Associate volunteers typically lead these groups from each community. They offer a place for the community to come together, learn, celebrate, vent, and work on solutions to workplace problems regarding our treatment. Interestingly, corporations that pursue DEI goals are the places people get the most exposure to education around marginalized communities. Most people spend their free time around others who are similar to them from a diversity standpoint. This makes the workplace a point of intersection where we (hopefully) work with people from all walks of life, so having resources, education, and teaching available is an essential aspect of the workplace regarding advocacy efforts.

What do we do if our workplace doesn't have ERGs? We create them. This task is challenging, so you'll want to gather a team to plan logistics and present the idea to company leadership to gain their support. Once you've created a document outlining the ERG's goals, structure, and guidelines, you'll want to find a senior individual to act as the sponsor of the ERG so the higher echelons of the company can advocate for it.

Creating a calendar of LGBTQIA events and days to acknowledge and celebrate throughout the year is your next step and the first significant deliverable of your programming. Remember, the goal is to create a community that can engage in workplace advocacy.

Beyond the calendar, there are many other milestones to meet:

- Hold events such as a Pride celebration.
- Create content and education that increases awareness within the workplace.
- Advocate for the executive committee within your organization to create equitable practices and work to retain diverse talent.

- As a workplace, join advocacy efforts within your city.
- Attend conferences that focus on DEI efforts in the workplace.
- Host speaking engagements with external LGBTQIA experts to talk with your associates.

Ultimately, the sky's the limit, but you'll need to plan for the long term and work to sustain involvement. Start small but create a plan to grow; you'll soon be pleased with your achievements. Pick up literature or bring in a consultant to help start these efforts within your firm, as this book does not afford me the space to dive into deep detail.

CONCLUSION

Friends, we've come to the end of *Advice From Your Trans Aunty*. I hope you found this information helpful, but most importantly I hope you found this book thought-provoking. As I stated up front, my goal has never been to tell people what to do but to give information that enables their growth, education, and agency.

I'm sure you have questions I didn't answer. Please know that it's impossible for me to answer every question in one book, or likely ever. Primarily, I wanted to cover what I feel are the basics of being trans and nonbinary, so some topics were not included. If you have a question you'd like my thoughts on, please feel free to contact me at www.ericavogel.com or through the social media links you'll find on my website. Your question may make it into an eventual second book from your trans aunty.

Before you go, I hope we can align on these essential themes:

1. There is no one way to be trans or nonbinary. As with cisgender people, there are infinite ways anyone can express gender.

2. Let people figure out their own expressions of gender, and leave the gatekeeping of someone's transness in relation to others in the dustbin.

3. You cannot truly embrace the trans and nonbinary community through a non-intersectional lens. We advance only when the most marginalized of us can step forward.

4. There are far more of us than most people are aware of, and yet you will still likely be the only trans person people know. Due to this fact, people will place an outsized burden on each of us to represent the entirety of the transgender community. We are not required to carry this mantle, but we may also not be given much choice.

5. Let people be who they say they are. Their life is not your life, and you will never be able to live their life for them.

In closing, one metric is most telling in how transgender people are doing: acceptance and love from the people around them. With acceptance from family, friends, community, and coworkers, we see that trans people thrive. The rates of mental health crises plummet, a positive outlook for the individual sharply rises, and most importantly an ability to feel that life can become manageable and stable takes root. When we make room at the table for transgender people, it's better for everyone involved. Because in my authenticity, you may just feel safe enough to embrace the best parts of yourself as well, whether you're trans or cisgender.

~ Your Trans Aunty

ACKNOWLEDGMENTS

Without the support and encouragement of many people in my life, this book wouldn't exist. Thank you for sticking with me through this effort.

To my wife Melissa, this book and my life wouldn't be as good without your partnership, support, love, and contributions.

To my friend Shikha Chivukula, thank you for having lunch with me in the Autumn of 2023 and giving me the idea for this book. I'll be forever grateful to you.

To Kathryn Thompson, Taryn Talley, and Leo Caldwell, thank you so much for reading my first draft and giving me feedback, as well as for your time, thoughtfulness, and most importantly your fierce friendship.

To Jenn Grace, Dawn Agnos, and Nancy Graham-Tillman at Publish Your Purpose, thank you so much for believing in this work and for being genuinely amazing partners.

I've been blessed to have some pretty amazing friends and family who've put up with me talking incessantly about this book while writing it. For your patience, I thank you.

Finally, to all of you who had the courage to ask me these questions, I would not be here without you. Thank you.

READER RESOURCES

WEBSITES

- **The Gender Dysphoria Bible**: genderdysphoria.fyi

  The purpose of this site is to document the many ways that Gender Dysphoria can manifest, as well as the numerous forms of gender transition, in order to provide a guide for those who are questioning, those who are starting their transgender journey, those already on their path, and those who simply wish to be better allies.

- **GLAAD**: glaad.org

  A nonprofit organization focused on LGBTQIA advocacy and cultural change, GLAAD works to ensure fair, accurate, and inclusive representation and creates national and local programs that advance LGBTQIA acceptance. Serving as a storyteller, media force, resource, and advocate, GLAAD tackles tough issues and provokes dialogue so that authentic LGBTQIA stories are seen, heard, and actualized.

- **National Center for Transgender Equality**: transequality.org

  The Center advocates to change policies and society to increase understanding and acceptance of transgender people. In the nation's capital and throughout the country, it works to replace disrespect, discrimination, and violence with empathy, opportunity, and justice.

- **The Trevor Project**: thetrevorproject.org

  As the leading suicide prevention and crisis intervention nonprofit organization for LGBTQIA young people, The Trevor Project provides information and support to LGBTQIA young people 24/7, all year round.

- **PFLAG** (formerly Parents, Families, and Friends of Lesbians and Gays): pflag.org

  PFLAG is the nation's largest organization dedicated to supporting, educating, and advocating for LGBTQIA people and those who love them.

- **WPATH**: wpath.org

  WPATH promotes evidence-based care, education, research, public policy, and respect in transgender health.

ARTICLES & BOOKS

- "Sexual Orientation and Gender Identity Definitions" by the Human Rights Campaign Foundation: https://www.hrc.org/resources/sexual-orientation-and-gender-identity-terminology-and-definitions
- "Survey of over 90,000 Trans People Shows Vast Improvement in Life Satisfaction after Transition" by NBC News: https://www.nbcnews.com/nbc-out/out-news/transgender-survey-transition-hrt-surgery-gender-affirming-rcna137563#
- *Testosterone: An Unauthorized Biography* by Rebecca M. Jordan-Young and Katrina Karkazis
- "Wheel of Privilege and Power," a graphic by the Center for Teaching, Learning & Mentoring Instructional Resources Knowledge Base of the University of Wisconsin-Madison: https://kb.wisc.edu/instructional-resources/page.php?id=119380

ABOUT THE AUTHOR

Erica Vogel is queer, a wife, a parent, and a member of a family with strong LGBTQIA roots. She has spent most of her life solving a wide variety of trials and tribulations as both a closeted and out transgender woman. Drawing from her experiences, her education, and her interactions with thousands of transgender people, she provides a point of view focused on personal agency as a transgender individual. Described as resilient, authentic, and fearless, she meets people where they are with grace and warmth.

Erica is a 20-year veteran of design and product management technology for start-ups to Fortune 500 companies. She holds a master's degree in business leadership and management and a DEI certification. Her recent tenures in tech also include serving on the national leadership team of corporate LGBTQIA employee resource groups with up to 5,000 members and as a board member of a transgender-focused tech nonprofit. She's a frequent public speaker on trans affairs both in and out of workplaces across the United States.

The B Corp Movement

Dear reader,

Thank you for reading this book and joining the Publish Your Purpose community! You are joining a special group of people who aim to make the world a better place.

What's Publish Your Purpose About?

Our mission is to elevate the voices often excluded from traditional publishing. We intentionally seek out authors and storytellers with diverse backgrounds, life experiences, and unique perspectives to publish books that will make an impact in the world.

Certified

Corporation

Beyond our books, we are focused on tangible, action-based change. As a woman- and LGBTQ+-owned company, we are committed to reducing inequality, lowering levels of poverty, creating a healthier environment, building stronger communities, and creating high-quality jobs with dignity and purpose.

As a Certified B Corporation, we use business as a force for good. We join a community of mission-driven companies building a more equitable, inclusive, and sustainable global economy. B Corporations must meet high standards of transparency, social and environmental performance, and accountability as determined by the nonprofit B Lab. The certification process is rigorous and ongoing (with a recertification requirement every three years).

How Do We Do This?

We intentionally partner with socially and economically disadvantaged businesses that meet our sustainability goals. We embrace and encourage our authors and employee's differences in race, age, color, disability, ethnicity, family or marital status, gender identity or expression, language, national origin, physical and mental ability, political affiliation, religion, sexual orientation, socio-economic status, veteran status, and other characteristics that make them unique.

Community is at the heart of everything we do—from our writing and publishing programs to contributing to social enterprise nonprofits like reSET (www.resetco. org) and our work in founding B Local Connecticut.

We are endlessly grateful to our authors, readers, and local community for being the driving force behind the equitable and sustainable world we are building together.

To connect with us online or publish with us,
visit us at www.publishyourpurpose.com.

Elevating Your Voice,

Jenn T Grace

Jenn T. Grace
Founder, Publish Your Purpose

www.ingramcontent.com/pod-product-compliance
Lightning Source LLC
Chambersburg PA
CBHW040135270326
41927CB00019B/3397